I0140123

FOR GOD'S SAKE,
Shut Up!

FOR GOD'S SAKE,
Shut Up!

Lessons for
Christians on
How to Speak
Effectively
and When to
Remain Silent

Brian Kaylor

Smyth & Helwys Publishing, Inc.
6316 Peake Road
Macon, Georgia 31210-3960
1-800-747-3016
©2007 by Smyth & Helwys Publishing
All rights reserved.
Printed in the United States of America.

The paper used in this publication meets the minimum requirements of
American National Standard for Information Sciences—
Permanence of Paper for Printed Library Materials.
ANSI Z39.48–1984. (alk. paper)

Library of Congress Cataloging-in-Publication Data

Kaylor, Brian.
For God's Sake Shut Up! : Lessons for Christians on How to Speak
Effectively and When to Remain Silent
by Brian Kaylor.
p. cm.
Includes bibliographical references and index.
ISBN 978-1-57312-485-0 (pbk. : alk. paper)
1. Oral communication–Religious aspects–Christianity.
I. Title.
BV4597.53.C64K39 2007
241'.672--dc22

2006038947

To my wonderful wife Jennifer,
for all her love and support.

Contents

Acknowledgements

Above all I wish to thank God for continual guidance and inspiration. While my goal has been to write what God would want communicated, I will not be so arrogant as to claim that everything I have written is directly from God. However, I hope it can be used to bring glory to God.

This book could not have been written without the encouragement and inspiration of many people. Most importantly is my wonderful and beautiful wife, Jennifer. She has encouraged and supported me throughout this process and offered invaluable suggestions and edits. Other family members have also provided encouragement and suggestions: my parents Doug and Carol Kaylor, my in-laws John and Ronda Credille, my sister Cristina Kaylor, my sister-in-law Pamela Credille, and my best friend Josh Gerrels and his family (who are like my second family).

I would especially like to thank everyone at Smyth & Helwys for providing me with this tremendous opportunity and helping me throughout this process, especially Keith Gammons, Griff Hogan, and Leslie Andres. I would also like to thank those who have given me writing opportunities that helped me to develop and improve my style: H.K. Neely and Jim Hill (of the Baptist General Convention of Missouri), and Bob Allen and Robert Parham (of the Baptist Center for Ethics).

There are a number of professors, pastors, and other individuals that have had a great influence on me and shaped my opinions. Anything you like in this book they probably taught me, and everything else I probably made up. Many professors have helped teach me about communication and the Christian faith, especially Bob Derryberry, Josh Compton, Mitchell McKinney, Rodney Reeves, Dan Cochran, Shannon Dyer, Mike Furham, Brett Miller, Scott Langston, Laura Cooper, and Linda Berry. I am indebted to their teachings as well as to that of many others at Jefferson City High School, Southwest Baptist University, and the University of Missouri. Several pastors and mentors have helped me to gain a better understanding about how to serve God and people, especially my grandfather Dorsey Derrick, Michael Olmstead, Todd Walker, Ron Hymer, Jim Shaver, Paul Harvey, Jim Albers, Jerry Fields, Nadeine Gold, Jim Walker, and Reuben Phelps.

Finally, I would like to thank the great people of Union Mound Baptist Church and the Baptist General Convention of Missouri for all the love, encouragement, and guidance they have provided me. We need more great Christians like those I have had the privilege to work with over the past few years.

Introduction
(But Please Read It Anyway)

Walking along the crowded streets of Chicago, I kept my head down as I fought the cold November wind. My hair was a mess, and my tie was flying behind me like a kite. I felt like an idiot for not bringing a coat—probably because I *was* an idiot. But, through it all, I was trying to look professional since I was there to present and listen to papers at the annual conference of the National Communication Association. I'm a communication "geek" (though I prefer the term "guru"), so don't say I didn't warn you!

Frankly, all I wanted to do was get inside to warm up and listen to the next set of studies on religious rhetoric. What? You think there is something more fun to do in Chicago? You've obviously never been to a conference like this. Anyway, I was deep in thought about the previous panel and future studies I couldn't wait to start researching in the library—when it happened.

"Repent now!"

Oh, great. A sidewalk preacher or—more accurately—a sidewalk screamer. This guy, however, had no breath control and kept pausing every couple of seconds, even in the middle of words. I wasn't sure if it was because of the cold wind or if he had been a smoker. Either way he was quite peculiar, even for a sidewalk preacher.

"Today is . . . the day of . . . the Lord. So . . . turn away from . . . your sins be . . . fore it is . . . too late, and . . . you find your . . . self in hell!"

I kept hoping he would then tell everyone to trust in Muhammad, Buddha, David Koresh, or anyone except Jesus. But no, he had to say "Jesus." Unfortunately, this guy even made the Branch Davidians seem sane. Like the Levite and the priest in Jesus' parable of the Good Samaritan, everyone was crossing to the other side of the street to avoid getting too close to the man. The dash was so quick you would have thought the red neon sign at Krispy Kreme had flashed on across the street (now *that* would have been heavenly!). Even I found myself scared I might catch whatever he had, or at least have him thrust at me some poorly written tract with stick figures being cast into hell. So I kept walking (on the other side of the street, of course) and hurried to my conference. I'd go back for the doughnuts later after I thought the coast was clear.

Later, this guy kept haunting my mind. I kept wishing I'd walked over to talk to him. I would have looked him straight in the eyes and said, "For God's sake, shut up!" I don't mean that profanely. I honestly believe his comments drove people away from God just as quickly as they were literally running away from him. Many people walking by probably left thinking Christians were kind of scary and kooky, not to mention unable to speak more than three syllables at a time.

Whenever Christians say or do stupid things, it damages unbelievers' perceptions of our Lord and Savior and may prevent them from ever accepting Jesus. We represent God in all we do and say. As we are reminded in 1 Peter 4:11, "If you speak, you should do so as one who speaks the very words of God."[1] That's a lot of pressure on us when you think about it. When we stick our foot in our mouth it not only makes us look bad, but it also hurts how people view God.

In May 2005, *Newsweek* accused some U.S. soldiers of flushing a Qur'an down the toilet. This article sparked protests and riots in the Middle East that resulted in more than a dozen deaths. The publication later retracted the story, but it was too late; people died because of the erroneous things written in the article. Likewise, Christians sometimes say misguiding and dumb things that ultimately drive away unbelievers and even split churches. This has resulted in the spiritual death of drastically more than the dozen affected by the *Newsweek* story.

Tonal Qualities

While the Chicago street yeller must have been tone deaf, I hope such a charge will not be leveled against me in this book (there will be plenty of other reasons to attack me). While the style of this book is a bit abnormal, I chose it deliberately. There are two quick aspects I should note about the tone. First, it may strike you as causal and informal at times (rather than a King James Bible style, it is more like the Living Bible). This style is intended to keep the discussion at a conversational level, which is how we need to communicate with other people. Too often it seems we are too worried about using big words and complex concepts to sound intelligent when we should focus on sounding natural. As a result, this book is written much as one would talk so it may serve as a role model for communication. Certainly it is *a* role model for communication; it will be up to you to decide if it is a *good* one.

The second aspect of the tone that may strike some as unusual is the sarcasm. While some may find it humorous, others may find it inappropriate at times. How can I be so sarcastic about religious leaders and their comments? Please remember that my attempts to have a little fun with situations do not mean I do not care about those I mention. Instead, this whole book is written because I care deeply about all Christians, even televangelists, and truly desire that all Christians, especially televangelists, would become more effective in reaching people with the love of Jesus.

The humor is simply my attempt to make this book enjoyable and educational—if you can make people laugh they are more likely to remember your point. Plus, laughing can keep you from crying. I will deal with issues of criticism in more detail in chapter 11. However, it is worth noting that I am not the only one to make the argument. Comedian Steven Colbert, formerly from *The Daily Show* and now host of *The Colbert Report*, explained,

> I love my church, and I'm a Catholic who was raised by intellectuals who were very devout. I was raised to believe that you could question the church and still be a Catholic. What is worthy of satire is the misuse of religion for destructive or political gains. That's totally different from the Word, the blood, the body, and the Christ. His kingdom is not of this earth.[2]

Colbert makes an excellent point (as he would say on *The Colbert Report*, he nailed it!) as he explains why someone can make fun of religious individuals without mocking God. In fact, it is because of my love for God that I satirize those who I feel are being poor ambassadors for God.

This book is a compilation of lessons I have learned from watching Christians in person and in the media make grave rhetorical errors. I don't claim to be an expert (just a "geek" and a "guru"), but I hope I can help you as you learn appropriate times, places, and ways to communicate your beliefs. This book deals with the pitfalls to avoid while planning what you will say and offers ways to be more effective in delivering your message.

I hope you will find these lessons on communicating effectively to be insightful and enjoyable. I urge you to recommend it to all your friends and enemies, and give it to everyone for Christmas. And please, if anyone happens to see the religious terror of the Chicago streets, give him a copy of the book for me.

Notes

1 All Scripture passages are taken from Today's New International Version.

2 "Quote of the Week," SojoMail, 23 August 2006, http://www.sojo.net/index.cfm?action=sojomail.display&issue=060823.

PART I:
Avoiding Common Mistakes

Chapter 1

God Gave You Two Ears and One Mouth: The Mistake of Not Listening to People

To answer before listening—that is folly and shame.
(Proverbs 18:13)

Comedian and fake news anchor Jon Stewart of *The Daily Show* appeared on CNN's *Crossfire* in October 2004 and unloaded a blistering critique of it and similar shows.[1] You know the type— the ones where two or four "grownups" sit around and yell at each other. He accused these yelling shows of "hurting America" and merely being "partisan hackery." He also suggested the shows were simply theater and compared them to professional wrestling (now that's a low blow). Stewart urged the hosts to change their ways (and Tucker Carlson to lose the bowties—yes, please!) as he asked, "Why can't we just talk—please, I beg of you guys, please." Three months later, when *Crossfire* was cancelled, CNN's president explained, "I agree wholeheartedly with Jon Stewart's overall premise."[2] Mark that one for the good guys, or at least the wise guys.

Occasionally on Stewart's *The Daily Show*, he includes a segment he calls "Moments in Television Punditry as Read by Children." In it kids calmly read the script from a yelling show where people were shouting, interrupting each other, and calling each other names. His point is clearly that he thinks these individuals are acting like children—actually worse than children. He's got a point. Why can't we sit down and calmly engage in dialogue? Of course, that means we would actually have to listen to the other side instead of interrupting them and putting them down. There's a lot of talking going on these days but sadly very little listening.

Unfortunately, it is not only politicians who enter these TV shouting matches. Christian ministers have also appeared to attack, yell at, and interrupt fellow Christians while the world watched. Here's part of an encounter from the July 13, 2004, edition of the *Tavis Smily Show* on National Public Radio between Reverend Jerry Falwell and Reverend Jim Wallis as the host attempted in vain to bring order. Notice how nothing is really accomplished because no one is listening to the other one:

> Wallis: Whoa, Jerry, Jerry, Jerry, I'm an evangelical Christian, too, and . . .
> Falwell: I know. But I want to ask you a question.
> Wallis: . . . you say Christians who take the Bible seriously . . .
> Falwell: Did you vote for Al Gore last time? Did you vote for Al Gore?
> Wallis: Jerry . . . [unintelligible]
> Smiley: Wait. Jim Wallis, Jim Wallis, go ahead.
> Falwell: You voted for a pro-choice candidate. How can . . .
> Wallis: . . . I'm going to talk, Jerry. You always interrupt people.
> Falwell: . . . an evangelical Christian . . .
> Smiley: Let—Rev. . . .
> Falwell: . . . vote for someone who's in favor of killing unborn babies?
> Smiley: Reverend Falwell, let me . . .
> Falwell: Come on, Jim, that's hypocritical.
> Smiley: Reverend Falwell . . .
> Wallis: Jerry, when you said . . .
> Smiley: . . . let me give Jim a chance to respond.

It goes on like that much longer, but I'm sure you get the point. On the November 28, 2004, broadcast of NBC's *Meet the Press* (this time an all-out Christian fight with Falwell, Wallis, Reverend Richard Land, and Reverend Al Sharpton), Falwell said Wallis was "anti-America" because of his different opinions on religious issues. Before the show had ended, nearly everyone involved had accused someone else of not reading or following the Bible. Ministers have also stepped into the *Crossfire* studio, and Falwell and Sharpton have even been co-hosts (really ring-masters) of the show. The ministers act as if the one with the best vocal chords and the cleverest sound bites wins. "Coming up next—watch these ministers enter the ring and hit each other over the head with chairs live on pay-per-view!"

These conversations are unhelpful because no one can get a full sentence out without being interrupted, and Christian leaders on national television aggressively attacking each other is embarrassing to Christianity. With that, our dirty laundry is hung up before the world as we present ourselves as mean-spirited, divided, and so sure we are right that we won't even listen to the other side. It's bad enough that we appear divided, but then the ministers will start quoting Scripture to attack each other. As a result, a nonbeliever may be left thinking that the Bible—and thus God—argues with itself or that both sides in the debate are hypocrites. I'm leaning toward the latter. These Christian leaders would have been wise to heed the admonition found in James 1:19—"My dear brothers and sisters, take note of this: Everyone should be quick to listen, slow to speak and slow to become angry."

Listen Up (or Sit Down)

While the concept of listening may seem simplistic, the fact is that most Americans are poor listeners and need to be reminded of the basics. The first step, to put it bluntly, is to shut your trap! Conservative commentator Cal Thomas, a former leader of the

Moral Majority, coauthored a book about the problems that occur when the church becomes too political. Near the end he offered advice about learning from the mistakes of himself and other Christian leaders like Falwell. The first item he gave was "First, more of us should shut up!"[3] That's why this chapter is first. Before we can become more effective speakers, we must learn to be quiet and listen.

If you were as talkative as I was as a child, you were probably told "God gave us two ears and one mouth, so we should listen twice as much as we speak." The Roman philosopher Epictetus originally made the statement 2,000 years ago using the term "nature" instead of "God." I later realized I had a good excuse for all my talking since I was partially deaf in both ears. But with hearing aids I am amazed at how much better I understand people. If you're having trouble listening to others, either get your hearing checked or place duct tape over your mouth.

While listening, attempt to understand what the speaker is saying and *then* evaluate it. For communication to be successful, there must be both a speaker and a listener, for it takes two to tango. (At least I think it does. I'm Baptist so I really don't know).

Plutarch chastised those who think they do not have to do anything as a listener:

> There are those who think that the speaker has a function to perform, and the hearer none. They think it is only right that the speaker shall come with his discourse carefully thought out and prepared while they, without consideration or thought of their obligations, rush in and take their seats exactly as though they had come to dinner, to have a good time while others toil. And yet even a well-bred guest at dinner has a function to perform, much more a hearer, for he is a participant in the discourse and a fellow-worker with the speaker.[4]

It sounds like he's describing the people who go to church merely to warm the pews. Our inability to hear a message from God is not necessarily the preacher's fault. After all, most of the people to whom the prophets and Jesus spoke didn't listen to or hear God's message (and then those people died—so let that be a warning to you!).

Too often we daydream or argue in our minds with a speaker without *really* understanding what the other person is saying. Thus, most incidents of miscommunication are actually the result of a failure to listen. But if we engage in empathic listening, which is when we truly try to understand the other's perspective and feelings, then we are more likely to understand the other person and their comments. Jesus had an advantage because he knew what people were thinking, and therefore he could appropriately respond. But since you're not a mind reader, then you must listen in order to understand people and what they think so that you can know what to say or not to say. Asking questions is also important if you aren't sure you completely understand the other person's point. While there might indeed be dumb questions (despite what your teachers told you), there are definitely dumb statements we might make because we were not listening.

Finally, when you are a listener, be sure to demonstrate respect for the speaker, remain open to what they are saying, and wait until they are finished to respond. Don't just listen; look like you're listening and care about what the speaker is saying. They probably won't think you're truly listening to them if you are shaking your head, making faces at them, doodling, or seeing if you can fit your fist into your mouth. Smile, make eye contact, nod your head, and even take notes to tell the speaker subtly that you care and are listening.

Hear and Now

Former Supreme Court justice John Marshall knew what he was talking about when he said, "To listen well is as powerful a means of communication and influence as to talk well." You may be wondering how listening really helps us communicate effectively, so listen up and I'll tell you. Kenneth Burke, one of the most prominent rhetoricians of the modern era, argued that "you persuade a man only insofar as you can talk his language by speech, gesture, tonality, order, image, attitude, idea, *identifying* your ways with his."[5] For Burke, identification was the key to persuasion. To identify with someone, you need first to listen so you understand them. By truly listening, you will be more likely to understand someone and then be able to relate to them in your speech. This is not to suggest that you lick your finger, check which direction the wind is blowing, and then say whatever people want to hear (unless you're a politician). Instead, you can adapt your message for a particular person or audience without going against your core beliefs. Many of the following chapters address how to do this. But before you can accurately and appropriately adjust your communication to be more effective, you must first listen and learn.

Listening not only helps you understand other people, but also being a good listener can help you gain the right to be heard. William Fay, author of *Sharing Jesus without Fear*, urged Christians to ask nonbelievers to share their spiritual stories. After being heard, the nonbeliever will likely be more open to listening to the Christian and their testimony. Communication scholar Michael P. Graves wrote about the power of silence among Quakers: "Words thus spoke 'out of the silence' take on significance *because* of the silence, because they have been 'weighed.'"[6] *New York Times* columnist Tom Friedman suggested that more listening is what is needed in today's political climate: "Listening is also a sign of respect. It is a sign that you actually value what the other person might have to say. If you just listen to someone first, it is amazing how much they will listen to you back."[7] Listening is powerful and helps you understand others and gain speaking opportunities.

In the weird and scary biblical book Revelation (poor John must have had nightmares for the rest of his life), we find letters from Jesus to seven churches. In each one, he states, "Whoever has ears, let them hear." We each have two ears, so it's definitely time to start hearing. Jesus healed the deaf in the New Testament, and I pray he will heal today's Christians as well. When Reverend Jim Wallis appeared on *The Daily Show* on January 18, 2005, he suggested that Jon Stewart was like the Hebrew prophets as he uses humor and telling the truth to make a point. I think Stewart's encounter on *Crossfire* confirms that. So go clean the wax out of your ears and start listening.

Notes

[1] For a complete transcript of the show, visit http://politicalhumor.about.com/library/bljonstewartcrossfire.htm.

[2] Robert P. Laurence, "Political hacks: CNN decides to cut 'Crossfire' from programming," *San Diego Union-Tribune,* 13 January 2005, E9.

[3] Cal Thomas and Ed Dobson, *Blinded by Might* (Grand Rapids: Zondervan Publishing House, 1999), 145.

[4] Courtland L. Bovee, *Contemporary Public Speaking* (San Diego: Collegiate Press, 2003), 81-82.

[5] Kenneth Burke, *A Rhetoric of Motives* (Berkeley: University of California Press, 1969), 55.

[6] Michael P. Graves, "One Friend's Journey," *Rhetoric & Public Affairs* 7/4 (Winter 2004): 518.

[7] Thomas L. Friedman, "Read My Ears," *New York Times,* 27 January 2005, 25.

Chapter 2

Teletubbies, Sponges, and Other Abominations: The Mistake of Not Picking Your Battles Wisely

The words of the reckless pierce like swords, but the tongue of the wise brings healing. (Proverbs 12:18)

If you've not yet decided that I'm fairly cynical at times, you probably will soon. Maybe that's one reason I appreciate Mahatma Gandhi's statement: "I like your Christ; I do not like your Christians. Your Christians are so unlike your Christ." Gandhi never became a Christian because the church rejected him due to the color of his skin. Yet, few men have displayed the humility and love of Jesus like Gandhi. How many others have we turned away?

If you're not feeling cynical yet, then think back to the summer of 2003. Yes, good old 2003, when everyone in the country was talking about a five-ton rock—the one with the Ten Commandments carved into it that then-Judge Roy Moore secretly hauled into the rotunda of the Alabama Supreme Court building in the middle of the night. Soon, hundreds of Christians showed up and rallied outside the courthouse for weeks. Many argued that if the Ten Commandments monument was removed, our government would become godless.

"Roy's Rock" apparently was magical, sort of a Jack and the beanstalk path straight to the throne of heaven. Alas, the monument was removed and Moore was kicked off the bench for breaking the law. After the ordeal, Moore and his rock (yes, he took the five-ton monument with him) traveled around the country as he spoke (and, of course, raised money) at various churches. With this, Moore attempted to continue his "rock star" status long enough to run for governor, though he was crushed in the Republican primary. When he started campaigning, he said it was because God told him to, which should make him ask why God is upset enough with him to set him up for such embarrassment (maybe it has something to do with that rock).

You may ask, shouldn't we stand strong and refuse to compromise? Alabama Baptist Charles McFatter argued that Moore was hurting the Christian witness and cause:

> More than likely this issue will not open the doors of heaven to a single individual soul. In that light it is not really very important. This fight becomes more important when we realize that in fact it may even have the exact opposite effect and serve to drive some souls away rather than attract individuals to the Christian faith.[1]

And Dr. Albert Mohler, president of Southern Baptist Theological Seminary, warned,

> We must learn to choose our battles wisely. The court-ordered removal of Alabama's Ten Commandments monument is a national tragedy and a travesty of law. But thoughtful and responsible Christian leaders must ponder whether this is the place to take our stand in a court-defying, go-for-broke effort. The recovery of a culture requires the stewardship of strategy as well as firmness of conviction.[2]

These men are right; just read a few of the thousands of arti-
cles and letters to the editor in newspapers across the country
and you'll hear comments from a lot of nonbelievers who were
turned off by the whole experience. Thus, this fight actually hurt
the work of God and may have driven people away forever. And
for what? A big rock. Actually, it's ironic that a bunch of
Christians basically worshipped the five-ton version of the Ten
Commandments despite the second commandment against
worshipping graven images. (Maybe we should focus on following the Ten Commandments instead of exerting our energy
carving them into every rock we can find.) Next time, let's build
our house upon the rock and not waste our time merely trying
to house a rock.

You've probably heard the saying "think before you speak."
Now that's a concept! I'd be happy if some Christians would
think at all, let alone before they speak. (I'll let you fill in names
of who you think deserve to be mentioned here, as long as you
don't say me). But I couldn't emphasize the importance of that
saying enough. This and the next couple of chapters will deal
with a few things to think about *before* speaking. First, let's discuss the importance of picking battles. Sometimes no matter
how much you want to say something, it is better to remain
silent and let it pass. This is a lesson I learned (though quite
slowly) over the years of talking back to my mom; trust me,
sometimes it's just not worth it to talk.

It's the Audience, Stupid!

The best way to decide when to speak and when to remain silent
is to consider the needs and thoughts of your potential audience.
If your audience doesn't understand your point, then the communication has failed. Not thinking about your audience prior
to speaking drastically increases your chances of failure. Dr.
Duane Litfin, president of Wheaton College and a preacher with
a Ph.D. in communication, explained the importance of think-

ing about your audience when planning a message: "But your choice should also weigh heavily the needs, interests, expectations, and intellectual abilities of your audience. Ignoring these factors in your choice and insisting upon pursuing your own interests alone is not only selfish; it is tantamount to committing rhetorical suicide."[3] If you don't consider the needs of your audience members, you may pick an inappropriate message or comment that hurts the Christian cause.

During the 1992 campaign, Bill Clinton's managers told him to stay on the topic of the economy and not allow himself to get sidetracked from it. They reminded him by stating, "It's the economy, stupid." For communicators, it's the audience, stupid. Stay on task and stay focused on your goal—sharing your beliefs with others. Had Judge Roy Moore considered this, he would not have launched his Ten Commandments campaign. It was not the message nonbelievers needed to hear. In reality, it was not the message Christians needed to hear either. But then again, "stupid is as stupid does" (or says).

While in high school I watched as a group of sincere but misguided Christians made the mistake of not choosing their battles wisely. The group decided to have a "Christian T-shirt Day," which on the surface seemed to be a good way to flood the halls with great religious messages. However, rather than simply picking a day and showing up in their best Christian T-shirts, they posted signs around school announcing the upcoming day to encourage everyone to participate. Of course, there was no rush of people who wanted to join the Christian club so they could wear the T-shirts (nothing says you're cool in high school like a shirt with "Turn or Burn!" plastered on the front). Then, as a joke, some students posted signs for "Pagan T-shirt Day" and controversy erupted.

Soon the school newspaper was publishing letters to the editor written by Christian students talking about how pained they were by the controversy. Shortly before all that occurred, a friend for whom I had prayed for quite some time started to seem interested in God and the Bible. We rode the bus together for more than thirty minutes each way, and he had started borrowing my Bible on the trips. However, when the Christian T-shirt editorials hit the newspaper with numerous inaccuracies and overly dramatic statements, he became disgusted. After that, he never asked to borrow my Bible again, and he never seemed as open to spiritual matters. What could have been a witnessing opportunity actually drove people away from God—all over a few cheesy T-shirts. Dr. Litfin said that ignoring your audience could be "rhetorical suicide," but it could also be spiritual homicide.

The Rabbit of Caerbannog

It is also important to stay on point during your speech or discussion. Many speakers, especially preachers, often have the bad habit of getting off point and chasing rabbits. My wife and I have a cute black cocker spaniel who loves to go on walks, which keeps us healthy and helps me avoid the "preacher belly" (which is why of the "seven deadly sins" gluttony is the one that is seldom mentioned from the pulpit). She'll be walking along just fine when suddenly she'll see a rabbit. The rabbit will run and our dog will quickly take off after it until she reaches the end of her leash and is suddenly jerked back as the rabbit escapes. Likewise, when we rhetorically chase rabbits, it accomplishes nothing, takes us off our path, wastes time and energy, and can actually hurt us or our cause.

I can think of a number of times when I wished a preacher or other Christian speaker was on a leash so I could jerk them back onto subject before they hurt their credibility or God's work by saying something dumb. (Can't somebody invent a "preacher leash?") I remember sitting at a preacher's conference in 2002 listening to Jerry Vines, pastor of a "supercenter church" in Florida. He was going along just fine with a pretty decent sermon when suddenly it happened—he chased a rabbit. You may have heard his comment, since it was repeated on national television and in hundreds of newspapers across the country. He called Muhammad a "demon-possessed pedophile." This was only seven months after 9/11, so religious tensions were high.

Don't get me wrong. I don't accept Muhammad or his teachings. But, aggressively attacking him is only going to drive Muslims and others away and paint Christians as hateful and mean-spirited. Nearly the entire conference, including most of Vines's sermon, was focused on inspiring statements about Jesus and positive and encouraging instructions to Christians. Yet, all of that was forgotten and ignored due to the controversy over this short and off-topic statement. Sadly, because Vines decided to take a trip down the rabbit hole, God's kingdom would have actually been better off if he had never said a word that day. Christian missionaries even wrote an open letter to him and others urging them to tone down the anti-Muslim rhetoric because it was hurting their ministry. Warren Larson, a professor of Islam and former missionary in Pakistan, explained that "saying that Muhammad was a demonized pedophile doesn't seem accurate or fair. Nor is it wise. We have a free press, but we have to use it with discretion."[4]

In the classic theological movie *Monty Python and the Search for the Holy Grail*, the crusaders are warned to beware of the vicious creature that guards the Cave of Caerbannog. When they get there, they discover it's just a little white rabbit. They ignore the warning and the rabbit kills a few of them. (Trust me, see the movie. It's a funny scene.) Unfortunately, a number of ministers and other Christians have seen their messages similarly destroyed because they chased a rabbit.

I could go on with examples of Christians wasting their time on meaningless debates and issues that don't have much eternal value. Jerry Falwell denounced Tinky Winky of the PBS children's show *Teletubbies*. James Dobson outed SpongeBob SquarePants as homosexual. (As a family counselor, shouldn't Dobson know that sponges are asexual). In Missouri, some

Christians decided to raise $8,000 to put the preamble of the state constitution on the wall of the capitol building since the document includes the word "Creator." These Christians were so excited because now God would be officially recognized on the capitol wall. Don't hold your breath waiting for someone to give their testimony about how they were reading the wall of the capitol and suddenly dropped to their knees and accepted Jesus.

Author and pastor Brian McLaren, a leader of the Emerging Church movement, put it well when he talked about the importance of choosing your battles wisely:

> The challenge for all fighters, of course, is to be sure that they find out what is now truly worth fighting against, and then be sure that they have something that is truly worth fighting for. . . . But unfortunately, so much of what we're currently fighting against . . . isn't the real enemy, and so much of what we're fighting for isn't the real prize.[5]

Just think how many Bibles and tracts could have been printed, how many churches or ministries helped, how many homeless people fed, etc. with that money wasted on the capitol wall or on "Roy's Rock." Think of all the people driven away by foolish comments about children's characters or other insignificant issues. Think of how many people like Gandhi were drawn to the teachings of Christ but repelled by Christians. That is the real abomination. Pick your battles wisely, or the next foolish crusade on which you embark may end in disaster with the rabid rabbits, or worse, with Moore bringing his five-ton idol to a church near you.

Notes

[1] Charles McFatter, "Ten Commandments," *Alabama Baptist,* 4 September 2003, http://www.thealabamabaptist.org/ip_template.asp?upid=1073.

[2] R. Albert Mohler, Jr., "The Battle of Montgomery: Where should Christians stand?" *Baptist Press,* 27 August 2003, http://bpnews.net/bpnews.asp?ID=16571.

[3] Duane Lifton, *Public Speaking: A Handbook for Christians* (Grand Rapids: Baker Books, 1992), 72.

[4] Stan Guthrie, "Waging Peace on Islam," *Christianity Today,* June 2005, 47.

[5] Brian D. McLaren, *A Generous Orthodoxy* (El Cajon CA: Youth Specialties, 2004), 184-85.

Chapter 3

An Inconvenient Truth:
The Mistake of Lying

*Their mouths are full of curses and lies and threats; trouble
and evil are under their tongues. (Psalm 10:7)*

I was placed on academic probation at seminary because of
lying. Not my lies, mind you, but those of an administrator. It
all started when I was writing a required essay to test English
proficiency. We were told that we would only be judged on
English abilities and not on content. I believed them and
decided to have a little fun and make the argument against a
recent denominational position (my devious streak does get me
in trouble at times—probably like this book will). I'm not talking about outright heresy or anything; many Baptists and other
Christians also believe this particular denominational position is
an inaccurate interpretation. However, this Baptist seminary did
not appreciate the essay, so they failed me and said I was not
proficient in English.

I still have the letter the seminary sent me—in which they
spelled my name wrong and made several grammatical mistakes—and I plan on framing it and hanging it on my wall
someday. The letter explained that I was being placed on academic probation and needed to take a remedial English course

before I could take any other classes (ironically, I am now writing about this while taking two doctoral-level English courses—the first English courses I have taken since receiving the letter). When I went to appeal, I was told there was no appeal. I then recounted to the administrator the exact steps he had explained right before we wrote the essay on how we could appeal. For some reason I had trusted him when he told us the process. He explained that it did not work that way anymore. With that, my seminary career ended. I have since studied at a state school, whose administrators I found more trustworthy in keeping their word. The whole ordeal was quite an education for a twenty-two-year-old (in fact, I learned more from this than I did in some of the seminary classes). Sadly, it seems that Christians are not always truthful people.

The biblical witness is clear on the issue of lying. In the Ten Commandments, we are told not to "bear false witness." In Proverbs 19:5, we are warned, "A false witness will not go unpunished, and whoever pours out lies will not go free" (thus our options are truth or consequences). In Jeremiah, God speaks out against the false prophets because of their lies. Paul urges us in Colossians 3:9, "Do not lie to each other, since you have taken off your old self with its practices." Numerous other verses also condemn lying. Yet, despite these clear admonitions against lying, it seems that nearly everywhere one looks, Christians are lying.

The problem is that when we lie, people no longer trust us. Archbishop John Foley once told Catholic communicators that when dealing with the media, "Never, never, never tell a lie."[1] He added, "Truth will always come out . . . Failure to tell the truth is a scandal, a betrayal of trust and a destroyer of credibility."[2] When people discover we have lied, we will not be trusted as much the next time we open our mouths. As Greek philosopher Aristotle explained, "Liars when they speak the truth are not believed." This becomes a problem because if we lie about some things, then people will be less likely to believe us about important things like the love of Jesus. As a result, Christians must keep their communication free of lies, deceptions, or exaggerations.

Consider the lies told by a couple of Christians during the Dover intelligent design court case. The judge ruled that Christians had lied under oath so that intelligent design could be taught in schools. The judge wrote, "It is ironic that several of these individuals, who so staunchly and proudly touted their religious convictions in public, would time and again lie to cover their tracks and disguise the real purpose behind the ID policy."[3] This judge makes an excellent observation that is ironic and sad. When Christians lie, it damages their reputation, making it less likely they will be trusted in the future. Therefore, we all need to take an oath to tell the truth, the whole truth, and nothing but the truth.

Where the Truth Lies

It seems that Christians are regularly getting in trouble for outright lies. In August 2006, pastor Steven Flockhart resigned from a Florida megachurch after it was exposed that he lied on his résumé regarding where he went to school.[4] During the 2004 election, the Reverend Al Sharpton continued to defend his involvement in the Tawana Brawley case from years earlier. Because of lies told during the Brawley episode, Sharpton was ordered to pay more than $300,000. In early 2006, Lutheran minister and Democrat politician Dean Johnson got caught in a controversy for lying to other pastors about statements made by Minnesota Supreme Court justices. The ethics investigation ended when Johnson agreed to apologize to the Senate and admitted to an "inaccurate statement" to the pastors, which is a nice way of saying he lied.[5] During the summer 2006 war in Israel and Lebanon, pro-war preacher John Hagee argued that America should support Israel no matter what (even, it seems, if Israel killed thousands of innocent civilians). To justify this

opinion, he argued, "Every word in the Bible was written by
Jewish hands."[6] He apparently has not read the books of Luke or
Acts.

These outright lies are generally easy to discover and are
clearly wrong. But they are not the only types of statements
Christians must work on avoiding; we also must be sure not to
be deliberately misleading. Even if one is technically accurate, if
the purpose is to mislead, it is still a lie (did you hear that Bill
Clinton?). It does not matter what the definition of "is" is, but
what your intention is. Philosopher Sissela Bok defines a lie as
"any intentionally deceptive message."[7] Thus, even if one uses
legal hairsplitting and is technically accurate but misleading,
then he or she is still lying.

The example of Bill Clinton is a worthy one to explore considering the amount of discussion it received among political
and religious circles. Clinton himself invoked religious language
during the ordeal. In the "Declaration concerning Religion,
Ethics, and the Crisis in the Clinton Presidency," a document
signed by nearly 200 religious and ethics teachers and scholars
during the Clinton scandal, the argument is made that the
truthfulness of our words is important. It reads, "We are particularly troubled about the debasing of the language of public
discourse with the aim of avoiding responsibility for one's
actions."[8] Drawing upon the *Catechism of the Catholic Church*,
William Buckley argued about the Clinton case that "lying is a
violence done to another" and "destructive to society."[9] The
Reverend Jim Wallis offered, "Stonewalling, and bending and
spinning the truth, are now, unfortunately, even further
entrenched as the way a president carries on public discourse."[10]

Unfortunately, it seems that Clintonesque twisting of language has not only infected our political discourse but our
religious communication as well. Late in 2006, influential evangelical leader Ted Haggard resigned as pastor of the largest
church in Colorado and as leader of the National Association of
Evangelicals after allegations were made that he used drugs and

paid a male prostitute for sex. At first he denied everything and—borrowing grammar from Clinton—stated, "I did not have a homosexual relationship with a man in Denver."[11] Since his language so closely matched Clinton's denial, it was not too surprising when Haggard started changing his story and admitting to some of the accusations. Sadly, this is not the only time such purposefully misleading language has been used.

Alexander Haig once stated, "That's not a lie, it's a terminological inexactitude. Also, a tactical misrepresentation." Such a line is oddly reminiscent of George Orwell's concept of "newspeak" in his novel *1984*. In the novel he exposes the intentionally misleading words through the fictional Newspeak language. For example, the word "joycamp" is used to describe a forced-labor prison in order to cover up the horrors of the place. Likewise, today's discourse often includes such lying terms. Consider "collateral damage," which sounds much nicer than saying we killed innocent people, or "abuse," which sounds much nicer than saying we tortured innocent people. Christians not only use these terms but also others that are misleading and thus lying. The point is that we should not avoid only the big or obvious lies. We must also beware of the language we use that misleads people.

What Lies Beneath[12]

Across the nation, embryonic stem cell research has garnered media attention and political discussion. Numerous religious leaders have jumped into the debate. In Missouri the issue became especially contentious, leading up to the 2006 election over a proposed state constitutional amendment and a U.S. Senate race with the candidates divided over embryonic stem cell research. Even though the measure and the candidate who supported it passed, opponents are already planning to bring another amendment to repeal this one in 2008.

In the midst of this fierce political battle, religious ideas and arguments played a fairly substantial role. So did religious money, as some Missouri Catholics and Baptists gave a couple hundred thousand dollars to defeat the amendment. The problem, however, was that many of these religious comments contained lies and deception. Politics seems to have trumped good doctrine. As a result, we are left merely with shallow and immature theology.

Christian speaker and frequent electoral punching bag Alan Keyes demonstrated this immature theology at a Springfield, Missouri, rally sponsored by Rick Scarborough's Vision America. Keyes told stem cell researchers, "God hates you."[13] Apparently his faith has not matured to the point of realizing that "God is love" (1 John 4:8) or that nothing can "separate us from the love of God" (Rom 8:39). What's next, mocking someone's Parkinson's disease? (Oh wait, Rush Limbaugh already did that.) Keyes should check out the warning in 1 John 4:20: "If we say we love god yet hate a brother or sister, we are liars." Sadly, it seems that when immature theology corrupts Christian discourse, it often results in lies being spread about others.

Just before the election, Rick Scarborough attacked John Danforth, an Episcopalian priest and former Republican senator with a pro-life voting record, for supporting the amendment. Scarborough accused Danforth of attacking Christians, "ignoring God's word," and "embrac[ing] secular humanism and reject[ing] absolute truth"[14] He ended by expressing his hope that Danforth would "have a conversion" and return "to the faith of our fathers" as found in the Declaration of Independence (the same faith that said slavery was okay).

Or consider the case of an ad that aired in opposition to the Missouri embryonic stem cell amendment. The ad, which featured Kurt Warner, Mike Sweeney, and Patricia Heaton, began with *The Passion of the Christ* star Jim Caviezel speaking in Aramaic with no subtitles. Since Missouri does not have a significant Aramaic-speaking population, the move appears to be an attempt to make sure viewers see Caviezel as Jesus. In fact, Caviezel's words, "You betray me with a kiss,"[15] are clearly intended to create the Christ comparison since that's his first line from *The Passion of the Christ.* Who needs the real and loving Jesus when we have a Hollywood actor to play the part? This ad included inaccurate information and attempted to mislead people by playing the "Jesus card," which is generally used when someone is unable to win an argument on the merits of the case.

A final case of immature theology is the deliberate attempts by some Christians to mislead and trick voters. Instead of being people of the Truth, some Christians have resorted to dirty politics and deception. Such actions can only be justified by a shallow and underdeveloped faith. Many mistruths and myths have been spread about the Missouri amendment. Religious leaders opposed to the amendment have also made false or exaggerated claims as they argued that the egg donation process was extremely dangerous, that embryonic stem cell research has been proven to be useless, and that the process being used was the same as the one used to clone "Dolly the Sheep." If you cannot beat something on its merits, then it appears that you can make stuff up.

However, these misleading comments do not appear to have been accidental. Kerry Messer, lobbyist for the Missouri Baptist Convention's Christian Life Commission, talked about some ads running in conjunction with the website 2tricky.org. Messer explained in the MBC's publication the *Pathway*, "The tricky ads are great because they're capitalizing on confusion . . . A confused voter generally is a 'No' voter."[16] Such a Christ-like response! Confuse them so you can trick them to vote how you want. When Christians begin to play worldly politics with such dirty strategies, then they have damaged their great calling. Instead of preaching the love of Jesus, some Christians seem to prefer tricks and deception. I want to make educated decisions, so I'm upset when I can't even trust the religious leaders.

Plato argued, "False words are not only evil in themselves, but they infect the soul with evil." This infection seems to occur when our immune system of good doctrine is weak. In Ephesians 4, Paul urges Christians to "become mature." He adds,

> *Then we will no longer be infants, tossed back and forth by the waves, and blown here and there by every wind of teaching and by the cunning and craftiness of people in their deceitful scheming. Instead, speaking the truth in love, we will in all things grow up into him who is the head, that is, Christ.*

Such advice is desperately needed today. Regardless of how one feels about embryonic stem cell research, all Christians should unite against immature theology and the lies that develop because of it. As George Orwell once posited, "During times of universal deceit, telling the truth becomes a revolutionary act." It is time to start the revolution! It is time for us to devote ourselves to being people of the Truth. It is time to stop the lies, the deceptions, and the exaggerations. As Christian and journalist Terry Mattingly urged, "For God's sake, let's tell the truth."[17] One should not have to go to seminary to figure this out.

Notes

[1] Terry Mattingly, "For God's sake, let's tell the truth," 25 December 2002, http://tmatt.gospelcom.net/column/2002/12/25.

[2] Ibid.

[3] The entire judgment can be read at http://www.pamd.uscourts.gov/kitzmiller/kitzmiller_342.pdf.

[4] Hannah Elliot, "West Palm Beach megachurch pastor resigns amid debt, resume expose," *Associated Baptist Press*, 28 August 2006, http://www.abpnews.com/1328.article.

[5] Pat Doyle, "Dean Johnson apologizes to his fellow senators," *Star Tribune* (Minneapolis), 28 March 2006, 1B.

[6] Abe Levy, "A champion for Israel," *San Antonio Express-News*, 23 July 2006.

[7] Sissela Bok, *Lying: Moral Choices in Public and Private Life* (New York: Vintage Books, 1999), 13.

[8] "Declaration concerning religion, ethics, and the crisis in the Clinton presidency," in *Judgment Day at the White House: A Critical Declaration Exploring Moral Issues and the Political Use and Abuse of Religion,* ed. Gabriel Fackre (Grand Rapids: William B. Eerdmans Publishing Company, 1999), 2.

[9] William J. Buckley, "Sex, lies and tapes: The case of Bill Clinton and Catholic teaching," in *Judgment day at the White House,* 142.

[10] Jim Wallis, "Clinton's repentance—and ours," *Sojourners,* November – December 1998, http://www.sojo.net/index.cfm?action=magazine.article&issue=soj9811 &article=981151&cookies_enabled=false.

[11] Terry Mattingly, "Timing, tapes and Clintonian grammar," *GetReligion,* 3 November 2006, http://www.getreligion.org/?p=2007.

[12] Parts of this section are drawn from a previous column: Brian Kaylor, "Embryonic theology," *Ethics Daily,* 6 November 2006, http://www.ethicsdaily.com/ article_detail.cfm?AID=8111.

[13] Tim Townsend, "An unusual alliance comes together," *St. Louis Post-Dispatch,* 22 October 2006, C1.

[14] Rich Scarborough, "John Danforth's attack on Christians," *WorldNetDaily,* 2 November 2006, http://www.worldnetdaily.com/news/article.asp?ARTICLE_ID =52742.

[15] Christian Bellantoni, "Jesus' words used vs. stem cell initiative," *Washington Times,* 26 October 2006, A03.

[16] Allen Palmeri, "Amendment 2's fate hinges on turnout," *Pathway,* 2 November 2006, http://www.mbcpathway.com/article17444c304396.htm.

[17] Mattingly, "For God's sake, let's tell the truth."

Chapter 4

Checking in for Ethics Rehab:
The Mistake of Not Considering
the Consequences

Even fools are thought wise if they keep silent, and discern-
ing if they hold their tongues. (Proverbs 17:28)

On October 6, 2002, Jerry Falwell created a controversy as he
attacked Muhammad on CBS's *60 Minutes*. He referred to the
Muslim prophet as a "terrorist" and "a violent man, a man of
war." He also contrasted Muhammad with Moses and Jesus:
"Jesus set the example for love, as did Moses, and I think
Muhammad set an opposite example." Didn't Moses personally
kill the slave master and then lead the Israelites as they slaugh-
tered whole nations? He sounds like "a violent man, a man of
war" to me. Maybe Falwell should have named a different
Judeo-Christian leader. Like Joshua, David, Samson, Gideon,
Paul . . . or maybe he should have just stuck with Jesus. That's
some good advice—stay focused on Jesus!

Unfortunately, Falwell's comments not only hurt the image
of Christians in America, but thanks to modern technology, *60
Minutes* is beamed around the world. After hearing Falwell's
interview, Muslims in India were outraged and began protesting

and rioting. At least five people were killed and sixty-seven injured.[1] So, as with *Newsweek* (mentioned in the introduction), Falwell's words have led to the deaths of innocent people. Perhaps it is time for the "Reverend" to start trying to *save* people, not *kill* them.

To his credit, Falwell did apologize for the statements. If it were not so tragic it would be ironic, since India is the same country to which shoe cobbler-turned-missionary William Carey, the father of the modern missionary movement, went to share the love of Jesus. Maybe it's time to let the shoe cobblers and other professionals start doing the talking and not the preachers.

Now, lest you think I'm pointing out the worst of American Christianity to make my point, the fact remains that Falwell is extremely influential and many people think he did nothing wrong. Shortly after the Falwell incident, I was in a religious course at the Baptist college I attended. Several of the students were adamant that Falwell did nothing wrong. I asked them about the fact that people died, but they were more concerned about telling "the truth" regardless of the consequences. But what is more important? Making your point even if it drives people away, or biting your tongue if that will help bring people closer to God?

You have probably heard the saying "Sticks and stones can break my bones, but words can never hurt me." While it may help a teased child feel better, there's really not much truth to the statement. The fact is that words are powerful, so they have to be chosen carefully. Jesus often pulled his rhetorical punches because he was more focused on changing peoples' lives. He could have yelled and berated the prostitutes and tax collectors. Instead, he told them how much they are loved and how they too can enter the kingdom of heaven (though I still think the IRS should be exempt from such hope).

Ethics 101

While most politicians seem to be talented public speakers, most seem to have flunked Ethics 101 (as many Christians must have, too). In reality, the two areas should be closely related. As Marcus Fabius Quintilian, one of the premier Roman rhetoricians, wrote,

> The orator then, whom I am concerned to form, shall be the orator as defined by Marcus Cato, "a good man, skilled in speaking." But above all he must possess the quality which Cato places first and which is in the very nature of things the greatest and most important, that is, he must be a good man.[2]

For Cato and Quintilian, you had to first be good/ethical and then learn how to speak well. Quintilian lived AD 35–86, which means he taught and wrote at the same time most of the books of the New Testament were written.

Quintilian also wrote, "The orator must above all things study *morality*, and must obtain a thorough knowledge of all that is just and honorable, without which no one can either be a good man or an able speaker."[3] Thus, Christians *should* be premier examples of good speakers. Maybe seminaries should teach more morality and less theology. For if skill alone is used to determine a good speaker, then we must hold up Adolf Hitler as a good example. But Hitler used his abilities to kill millions of innocent people, while the church basically went along with it or even supported it. Tragically, the messages of Christians today sometimes also lead to death, even if unintended.

For all politicians and preachers, here is a quick reminder about ethical communication—tell the truth! Unfortunately, many Christians twist the facts to push their agenda. Shortly after 9/11, Falwell remarked on Pat Robertson's *700 Club*, "I really believe that the pagans, and the abortionists, and the feminists, and the gays and the lesbians who are actively trying to make that an alternative lifestyle, the ACLU, People For the

American Way, all of them who have tried to secularize America. I point the finger in their face and say you helped this happen."[4]

He called Muhammad a terrorist but said the 9/11 terrorist act happened because of pagans, abortions, feminists, etc. He later apologized for the statement (it might be easier if he just mentioned all of his sayings for which he *doesn't* need to apologize). Jesus said, "I am the way, the *truth*, and the life." If Jesus is the truth and we twist the truth, what does that mean we're doing? Yet it seems that Falwell and other Christian speakers often rely on the "twist & shout" strategy of persuasion. But it's the Truth that will set you free.

Another ethical note to remember is not to plagiarize. Journalists from Jayson Blair at the *New York Times* to Jack Kelly at *USA Today* learned this lesson the hard way. Kelly, for the record, was an outspoken evangelical Christian and often headlined Christian press conferences. Some Christians complain of an anti-Christian bias in the media, and now I guess the media will complain of an anti-truth bias among Christians.

But perhaps the most common place of plagiarism is the pulpit, and sadly many preachers and theology students joke about it. While using someone else's words may help church members hear a better sermon than they would have from the preacher, it can also greatly embarrass the church if uncovered. There have been several occasions when pastors have been exposed in the secular press and forced to resign. Often they found sermons in preaching magazines or online. If you're a really pathetic preacher, try www.desparatepreacher.com, where you can find links for sermons, sermon illustrations, and women. Yes, for the preacher in need of a sermon there are links for dating services. If you have absolutely nothing on which to preach, then try reading the Sermon on the Mount as is to people—can you really do any better than Jesus' sermon anyway?

Reverend Dean W. Nadasdy has told the story of being on vacation and hearing a sermon he had written being delivered by another minister without acknowledgment. The guy even told Nadasdy's personal family story as his own, at which point Nadasdy's children looked up and said, "Hey, that's our story!"[5] You know you live a boring life when you have to borrow other people's stories. Sadly, this is not an isolated incident, as I have heard numerous other stories of preachers hearing their own sermons.

Here's Your Sign

American essayist and editor Norman Cousins once said, "Wisdom consists of the anticipation of consequences." Before you speak, you should stop and think about what may happen as a result of what you plan to say. This consideration should be twofold: is your purpose helpful, and is there an unintended message people may take from it? If you do not consider the consequences of your words, you may be playing a rhetorical version of Russian roulette.

In May 2005, Creighton Lovelace, pastor of Danieltown Baptist Church in North Carolina, placed a hateful message on the church's sign. It was posted immediately following the *Newsweek* controversy about the Qur'an allegedly being flushed down the toilet. The sign read, "The Qur'an needs to be flushed." While initially refusing to remove it or apologize, Lovelace did eventually do both. However, the damage was already done. Christians were portrayed across the country and the world as hateful, bigoted, and stupid. If only he would have thought ethically about the potential consequences. If only he would have thought at all. After being appropriately criticized by Southern Baptist leaders, Lovelace and the church left the Southern Baptist Convention to become an independent Baptist church.

We need more thinking Christians. Regardless of how badly you want to say something, stop and think to make sure it is the best thing to say. Ask yourself if it is ethical, if it is appropriate, and, most importantly, if it will help the cause. If not, for God's sake (and your own), remain silent. Bill Engvall recorded a song in which he wishes dumb people wore a sign so the rest of us would be warned of their stupidity. After listing someone doing something dumb, he says, "Here's your sign." I wish I could say to individuals such as Lovelace, Falwell, and others, "Here's your sign." It's time to think wisely about what we say. As evangelical preacher Tony Campolo wrote about Falwell and others,

> On simply pragmatic grounds, we have to ask what good we accomplish with such inflammatory rhetoric. And we have to ask if those outspoken Christian leaders who claim to be committed to winning Muslims to Christ have given any consideration to the possibility that their accusations might make Muslims even more resistant to the Christian gospel.[6]

Cato, one of the Romans mentioned earlier, once stated, "He approaches closer to the gods who knows how to be silent, even though he is in the right." Likewise, there are numerous occasions when Christians would be more helpful if they would remain silent and avoid disastrous consequences. As the famous saying goes, "when in Rome do as the Romans do." The Roman rhetoricians taught us to think ethically and consider the potential consequences of our words. Many Christians would be wise to speak like the Romans, whether they are in Rome or not.

Notes

[1] "5 Die in India During Protests Over Falwell," *New York Times,* 12 October 2002, A5.

[2] Quintilian, *Institutes of Oratory,* trans. H. E. Butler, in Readings in Classical Rhetoric, ed. Thomas W. Benson and Michael H. Prosser (Davis CA: Hermagoras Press, 1988), 118.

[3] Earnest Brandenburg, "Quintilian and the Good Orator," *Quarterly Journal of Speech* 34/1 (February 1948): 23.

[4] For a complete transcript of the show, visit http://www.commondreams.org/news2001/0917-03.htm.

[5] Story told in a Concordia Publishing House e-newsletter that can be found at http://www.cph.org/Newsletter/Churches/03/sep/pulpit.asp.

[6] Tony Campolo, *Speaking My Mind* (Nashville: W Publishing Group, 2004), 139.

Chapter 5

Oops: The Mistake of Not Avoiding Logical Fallacies

The tongue of the wise adorns knowledge, but the mouth of the fool gushes folly. (Proverbs 15:2)

On April 24, 2005, several prominent Christian leaders gathered together for Justice Sunday, a political rally held in a Baptist church on Sunday night. Instead of preaching the gospel that Sunday evening, Christian leaders gathered to rally against Democrats who were filibustering Bush's judicial nominees. They accused the Democrats of filibustering "people of faith" (apparently the 205 nominees already approved were atheists). Unfortunately, the event was followed by two sequels and provided much material for comedians and commentators to demonstrate the inconsistencies and poor logic of some Christian leaders.

Al Mohler, one of the speakers at the political church rally, explained, "This is a church that is established upon the gospel of the Lord Jesus Christ. The main message we want to communicate is that we want to see all persons come to know the Lord Jesus Christ as Savior." Sounds good, so start doing it! Apparently, Mohler and the others at the rally thought that ending an obscure Senate rule allowing people to talk a lot would spark a great spiritual revival across America. Oops. Clearly there are some problems with his logic.

Sadly, this incident is not an isolated case of poor argumentation. This chapter describes six types of logical fallacies you should avoid in order to make sure your arguments are better developed and more likely to win people over. After all, faulty reasoning can hurt your credibility and therefore your cause. Justice Sunday did not bring "justice," but it did provide many examples of logical fallacies. Here are a few types of arguments you should try to avoid.

Taking on "The Man"

The first fallacy is that of *ad hominem*, which is Latin for "to the man" (or woman). This problem occurs when someone attacks their opponent and not the arguments. For instance, at the Justice Sunday rally Bill Donahue of the Catholic League argued for judicial reform in order to prevent "the most insane idea I've heard in my whole life, of two men getting married. I mean that's something you expect in the asylum, quite frankly." Just moments before that statement, he urged everyone in the debate to "keep it civil." That's some good advice—for Donahue especially. Believing homosexuality is a sin is one thing, but aggressively and falsely attacking homosexuals is quite another (whatever happened to "love the sinner, hate the sin"?).

The real problem with Donahue's argument is how easily it can be refuted. If you know one homosexual who is not mentally ill—which I do—then Donahue is clearly wrong. Oops. Attacking a person does not disprove their stance on the actual issue. Just because Jim Bakker stole money from people (and married a crazy-looking woman) does not mean he was wrong when he urged people to turn their lives over to Jesus. Simply calling someone a "cheater," "liar," "crazy-looking," or "adulterer" does not win the debate for you. This is especially troublesome when Christians start throwing mud at each other. Leave the man (or woman) alone and stick to the point.

Running in Circles

Another logical fallacy is the use of circular reasoning. In this argument, one makes a claim and then "supports" it with the claim, thus not proving anything. For instance, a classic example in many speech textbooks is this: the Bible is the Word of God because the Bible says so. This argument can quickly get you rhetorically spinning in circles.

You claim, "The Bible is the Word of God."

Someone else asks, "How do you know this?"

"Because the Bible says so," you answer.

"But why does that matter?"

You respond, "Because the Bible is the Word of God."

They ask, "How do you know this?"

Oops. And on and on the discussion could go in a circle, making you dizzy. I'm not saying the Bible is not the Word of God—in fact, I believe it is. But, when talking to someone with a different worldview who doesn't believe the Bible is the Word of God, the Bible is not going to carry a lot of weight. You need to bring in outside support to convince them of the truths of the Bible.

If you're looking for a good starting point, tell them about how God has changed your life, because that's hard to argue with (unless you don't live like you've been changed, and then please just keep your mouth shut). Just because you claim something does not make it true, as demonstrated by many politicians and televangelists. So attempt to find examples or facts to support your arguments.

To Infinity and Beyond!

The next fallacy is known as *reductio ad absurdum*, which means "extending an argument to absurd lengths." The absurd extension is basically when one exaggerates their point (fishermen and preachers are especially bad at this—and if your preacher's a fisherman, you'd better watch out). Consider a couple of statements made at Justice Sunday by Focus on the Family founder James Dobson. Early in his speech he said this about the fight to end the filibuster: "My goodness, I just cannot imagine anything more significant than what we're about to do." Nothing more significant? What about leading someone to Christ, helping teach families how to function better, or feeding the homeless and reducing poverty (or even scrubbing the church toilets)? He could have simply called it an important event. But calling it the most significant undermines his credibility and his point.

Later in the speech, Dobson continued his use of hyperbole by arguing that stopping the filibuster was important "because the future of democracy and ordered liberty actually depends on the outcome of this struggle." He could have called it important because our democracy would be better with this change. However, considering our nation has survived a civil war, two world wars, slavery, the assassination of four presidents, the resignation of a president, and numerous scandals, I think we might survive a little more talking in the Senate. By the way, if you don't remember, a few senators got together and stopped the attempts by Dobson and others to remove the filibuster. Playing "Chicken Little"—acting as if certain matters are of life and death when they are not—can only hurt your credibility and the believability of your arguments. Oops. So don't exaggerate or make claims you can't prove.

"I Wish I Had a Brain"

The next logical fallacy to consider is the straw man argument. This occurs when someone constructs a similar but weaker version of their opponent's argument and then destroys it. This approach gives the impression that the speaker has proven their opponent wrong, but in reality they have not. Think about it like this: I'm not a big guy, so I probably couldn't physically beat up many people. But, to make myself feel better, I build a strong-looking man out of straw and then beat the thing to pieces. This doesn't mean I'm He-Man, just misleading.

During the Justice Sunday rally, Chuck Colson attacked Democrats who had attacked the purpose of the rally. He stated, "When liberal senators like Senator Kennedy and Senator Reid were saying, 'What are people of faith doing getting involved in this process?' We shouldn't be involved because we're Christians?" He claims the rally leaders were attacked for being Christians getting involved in the process, but that is not what Kennedy or Reid said.

Senator Harry Reid actually said, "In America, we are in a democracy, not a theocracy. God does not take part in partisan politics."[1] He was not saying Christians should not speak out, but that Christians must not impose their beliefs on others or claim to speak authoritatively for God, especially on non-scriptural matters (I don't recall the commandment that states, "Thou shalt not filibuster judicial appointees"). Senator Ted Kennedy actually argued that the event violated the historic separation of church and state, which is not that Christians should remain silent but that government must not become too religious and religion should not become too political. Thomas Jefferson originally penned the phrase in a letter to Baptists who feared the state would support one religious group and its beliefs over the others. Ironically, it is now the Baptists who lead the charge against this historic principle (back then they were the minority who wanted separation; now that they are the majority they want to unite church and state and be in charge).

These and other opponents of Justice Sunday were not saying Christians should not speak out, but that it is wrong to suggest that ending the filibuster is God's will or that if you support the filibuster you are not a faithful Christian. After all, both Kennedy and Reid would consider themselves religious, and Reid is pro-life (which the speakers at Justice Sunday seem to think can only happen if one is a Republican/Christian). Oops. Not only does Colson not defeat the *actual* arguments of his opponents, but he is unethical as he misrepresents their claims.

In *The Wizard of Oz*, the Scarecrow (the classic straw man— remember how easily the flying monkeys tore him up!) explains to Dorothy that he does not have a brain, only straw. She asks how he can talk if he doesn't have a brain. He says he doesn't know and then adds, "But some people without brains do an awful lot of talking." Unfortunately, Christians sometimes use poor logic that would seem to prove his statement.

Painting with a Broad Stroke

Another logical fallacy is hasty generalization. You might have heard this called stereotyping or painting with a broad stroke. People use this approach to label a large group of people or things as being basically the same. Generalization is a fallacy because it remains impossible to identify every single individual in a group as being the same as every other one. Just because most televangelists seem more concerned with money than the gospel, have shallow or incorrect theology, and wear cheesy suits does not mean *all* of them do (granted, I cannot think of one who doesn't fit in that generalization, but I'm sure there's at least one). The key is to focus on each person or group on their own merits and not simply label with a stereotype or hasty generalization.

During the Justice Sunday rally, several of the speakers rushed to hasty generalizations, especially concerning judicial decisions with which they disagreed. In particular, the speakers pointed to the Terri Schiavo case—the Florida woman in a persistent vegetative state who died after her feeding tubes were removed—as proof of problems with the judiciary. Bill Donahue spoke about "anti-Christian bigotry" in the judiciary and then argued, "because if Christians can't get that voice out there in favor of marriage, family, and life, the life of a child to be born, and the life of Terri Schiavo to have feeding tubes, then we're all finished." A few days after the rally, Focus on the Family's CitizenLink posted an article that stated, "What kind of judges do liberals want? Those like the ones who allowed Terri Schiavo to be starved and dehydrated to death."[2]

These arguments seem simple enough until you look at the facts. Who was this godless liberal judge who "killed" Terri Schiavo? Judge George W. Greer. Guess what? He's not only a Republican, but he's also a longtime Southern Baptist (the same denomination of the church that hosted the event). The main judge in the case was a conservative evangelical Christian. Oops. You need to be careful about making hasty generalizations because you could be way off base.

Since I've already brought up the Schiavo case, allow me to make a slightly off-topic observation. Not only was the Justice Sunday crowd wrong with their hasty generalization that godless liberal judges led to the Schiavo decision, but they were also wrong with their rhetoric throughout the case. Without any evidence whatsoever, many Christian leaders started accusing Schiavo's husband of having beat or hurt her to cause her condition. That's a classic: if you disagree with someone's position, call them a wife beater and a murderer.

Christians also claimed that Schiavo was not in a persistent vegetative state and that she was responding to people by looking at them. Later, the autopsy proved that she was in a persistent vegetative state and that she was blind and thus could not have actually looked at her family. Oops. Rather than apologizing for being wrong, Christian leaders renewed their accusations against Schiavo's husband (if at first you don't succeed, lie, lie again).

At one point in the mess, President Bush claimed, "it is wisest to always err on the side of life."[3] That sounds good and is close to how Christians should act. We should err on the side of *eternal* life. Consider this: Terri Schiavo was a Christian and is in heaven today. Her husband is not a Christian, and I believe he will probably never be because of the inaccurate, hateful, un-Christlike, and plain stupid things Christians said about him. In their attempt to save a dead person, Christians have likely eternally killed her husband. Oops.

Additionally, numerous Southern Baptist leaders publicly and harshly attacked Judge Greer. Because of these attacks, Greer left the church. Another victim of "friendly fire." Oops.

Majority Rules, Minority Drools

The final logical fallacy is called *ad populum*, which is Latin for "to the people." This is the claim that since a majority of people are doing or believing something, then it *must* be correct. Hopefully, you know this majority rules, or bandwagon, type of appeal is not logical. Whenever I wanted to do something because everyone else was doing it, my mother would ask, "If all your friends jumped off a bridge, would you?" Of course, I would then respond, "It depends on how high the bridge is." But I got the point. It's okay to be different.

Politicians use this claim about half of the time—the half when the polls support them. Actually, it's funny to hear a senator argue that the will of the people should be preserved and so everyone should vote for his or her bill, and then in the debate over the next bill that senator will argue against an issue even though most people support it. The Justice Sunday guys were no different. They cited polls that supported their stances on social issues but ignored polls saying most people did not support removing the filibuster with the "nuclear option." Oops.

Just because everyone supports you on an issue does not mean you are correct. Remember, majority mob rule in the

Bible led to forty years of wandering in the wilderness. Jesus and his followers were clearly in the minority among the religious and political leaders of his day. Christians used to be the persecuted minority. Now in America we're the majority that persecutes the minorities. Instead of relying on poll numbers, we must return to reading Scripture and doing God's work.

I could identify many other logical fallacies. For instance, in chapter 1 I mentioned Jon Stewart's attacks on the yelling shows for polarizing America. Those shows fall prey to the "false dichotomy" fallacy by suggesting there are only two sides to an issue, when in reality there are usually numerous perspectives. But these fallacies are among the most common ones Christians seem to use. Basically, the key to avoiding these and other fallacies is to *think*.

In the movie *Independence Day*, the word "oops" is said several times. At one point Will Smith's character hits a wall with the alien spaceship and says, "Oops." After figuring out what went wrong, he looks at Jeff Goldblum's character and says, "What do you say we try that one again, huh?" Goldblum responds, "Yes, yes, without the oops." Later in the movie, Smith gets upset at Goldblum for not telling him about something. Goldblum responds, "Oops." To which Smith states, "We're gonna have to work on our communication!" That's good advice! As Christians we have had too many "oops" moments because of poor arguments and the use of logical fallacies. Let's try to communicate without the oops.

Notes

[1] David D. Kirkpatrick and Carl Hulse, "Democrats Accuse Frist of Exploiting Religion," *New York Times*, 16 April 2005, 11.

[2] "Time is Running Out to Strike a Blow Against Judicial Tyranny," *CitizenLink*, 28 April 2005, http://www.family.org/cforum/extras/a0036344.cfm.

[3] Anne E. Kornblut, "After Signing Schiavo Law, Bush Says 'It is Wisest to Always Err on the Side of Life,'" *New York Times*, 22 March 2005, A19.

Chapter 6

Breaking the Body of Christ: The Mistake of Using Inappropriate Metaphors[1]

With the tongue we praise our Lord and Father, and with it we curse human beings, who have been made in God's likeness. . . . Can both fresh water and salt water flow from the same spring? My brothers and sisters, can a fig tree bear olives, or a grapevine bear figs? Neither can a salt spring produce fresh water.
(James 3:9, 11-12)

In July 2006, Missouri Baptist Convention (MBC) attorney Michael Whitehead spoke with Dick Bott on the radio program *The Complete Story*. The two discussed the MBC's lawsuit against five Missouri Baptist institutions. During the show, Bott said that trustees at Windermere Baptist Conference Center were "rogue elephants." Whitehead responded by saying, "Yeah."

Such a line is completely inappropriate. A "rogue elephant" is a violent elephant that has left the herd, thus it is a misnomer to speak of "rogue elephants."

In Africa, these wild animals are considered extremely dangerous. Thus, people kill them. Tarquin Hall details the hunt of a rogue elephant in his book *To the Elephant Graveyard.* In it he is told, "You can't put such a rogue elephant in a cage, you can't tie him to a post, you can't pacify him or reason with him, and he can't be trained. He has to be killed or he will kill."[2]

Yet, Bott used and Whitehead agreed with the metaphor of "rogue elephants" to describe fellow Christians. While they were not suggesting the Windermere trustees should literally be killed (at least I do not think they were), the use of such a metaphor suggests an inappropriate view. It dehumanizes people by comparing them to animals and inaccurately compares a disagreement over control of assets to the killing of people (it would be more accurate to compare the disagreement to a complete waste of time and money). It is also inappropriate because it compares fellow Christians with creatures that are hunted down and killed.

Paying for Metaphors

Why does it matter what the radio talk show host said? Is it not just rhetoric? In actuality, it is important because the metaphors we use offer insight into our thinking. When we choose one word over another, it could drastically change how we think about and act toward that which is being described. To call someone a "rogue elephant" is important because of the implications of the metaphor—that those so described are being viewed as animals that deserve to be killed.

In their book *Metaphors We Live By*, George Lakoff and Mark Johnson argue that a "metaphor is not just a matter of language, that is, of mere words."[3] They add that metaphors not only impact "how we perceive" and "how we think" but also "what we do"[4] (thus, we are what we say). Consider the difference Lakoff and Johnson offer between calling an argument "war" and calling it "dance." With the first metaphoric framework, we "win or lose arguments" and "see the person we are arguing with as an opponent."[5] With the second, we see it as a place "where no one won or lost, where there was no sense of attacking or defending."[6]

Simply changing our wording—and thus our view—of arguments from that of "war" to "dance" would drastically change how we act in arguments. As Lakoff and Johnson explain, people in these different worldviews "would view arguments differently, experience them differently, carry them out differently, and talk about them differently."[7] The words we use impact how we view the world and therefore how we treat others within it (as the old peace slogan goes, "make dance not war").

Thus, when Bott referred to his brothers and sisters in Christ as "rogue elephants" and Whitehead agreed with him, they provided important insights into how they viewed their brothers and sisters and how they would treat them—as animals to kill. They would not literally kill them, but it seems that the two would do whatever they could to hurt the ministries (such as suing them and calling them names on a radio program). Such a metaphorical worldview is not only inappropriate and unbiblical, but it has also led to inappropriate and unbiblical actions.

It is important to understand contextual and cultural differences as language—especially metaphors—carries different meanings for different time periods or cultures. After all, we constantly need to translate the Scriptures into current vernacular (despite what some may seem to claim, Paul did not write in King James English). Brian McLaren argued in a *Sojourners* article that Christians should attempt to find new metaphors for "kingdom of God" that are more relevant and easier to understand. He argued that the language has lost its "urgent political, religious, and cultural electricity"[8] and often communicates the opposite message of what it originally intended. As a result, he suggested other possible metaphors to use: dream of God, revolution of God, mission of God, party of God, ecosystem of God, and dance of God. Some of those are unlikely to catch on, and others are likely not to be accepted by many religious leaders. However, even if you do not like any of his suggestions, McLaren still does a great job of reminding us that we need to think seriously about the metaphors we use. As McLaren explained, "Whatever metaphors we choose will likely have a limited shelf life, and each will be open to various misunderstandings—just as Jesus' own metaphors were."[9] Because of the importance of the message, it is important to consider how we describe it.

A credit card company had a television commercial fairly recently that featured New England Patriots quarterback Tom Brady and members of his offensive line eating out at dinner. In it, the members of the offensive line explain to Brady how they each represent a different feature of the credit card designed to protect him. When the bill comes to Brady, he asks the others, "Do metaphors pay?" They laugh and tell him no. While metaphors may not pay at dinner, if we are not careful we may end up paying for our metaphors.

Attack of the Killer Metaphors

Metaphors we use are important, because as Lakoff argued, "Metaphors can kill."[10] He explained that before a war begins the nation's leaders often begin to set the stage with the metaphors they use to describe the enemy. Sometimes this involves dehumanizing the others by comparing them to animals. As with the "rogue elephants" metaphor, Christians often choose inappropriate ways to talk about other Christians. Perhaps one of the worst examples came in the midst of the Episcopalian conflict about homosexual bishops. The Reverend Paul Zahl, dean of the conservative Trinity Episcopal School for Ministry in Ambridge, Pennsylvania, compared the possible election of a gay bishop to "a terrorist bomb."[11] With this metaphor, there can be no working together because one does not hold hands with a terrorist bomb.

Regardless of which side of the debate one takes, such a metaphor is irresponsible. In response to Zahl's remark, Susan Russell, president of Integrity, argued,

> Paul Zahl's comments comparing the election of a gay bishop to a "terrorist bomb" is hate speech that has no place in any faith-based discourse. Such language does nothing to advance our public discourse, does everything to further polarize and alienate and is antithetical to the love God calls us all to offer each other.[12]

Jim Naughton, director of communications for the Episcopal Diocese of Washington, put it well when he said, "Terrorism, as we know, takes lives. It shatters bodies, families and societies. . . . When you use a phrase like 'terrorist bomb,' you conjure up images of torn limbs, devastated bodies, blood, lots of blood. It is not a metaphor one should use lightly."[13]

Not only should the "bomb" metaphor not be used lightly, but it is one that should not be used at all among Christians (unless we are talking about literal terrorist bombs or the *Left Behind* movies).

Unfortunately, this outrageous comment is not an isolated case. We Christians like to attack each other with colorful metaphors, often involving death. On the CBS Evening News broadcast of September 21, 2006, Family Research Council president Tony Perkins wildly compared moderate Christians to road kill. He stated, "Well, you know, what's in the middle are usually dead cats and skunks that have been run over. That's what's usually in the middle of the road." The next day, his organization hosted a meeting to teach conservative Christians how to help the Republicans win elections (apparently in his attempt to *run over* the opposition).

However, this metaphor is problematic for a number of reasons. First, it wrongly compares moderate Christians to dead animals. This metaphor also overplays the differences between liberal and conservative Christians. In the metaphor, they are going in exact opposite directions. Though often with different ideas on issues, it would not be fair to say the two camps are headed in exact opposite directions. Thus, with Perkins's metaphor there is no chance to hold hands and work together on an issue. With this metaphor in mind, it should not be surprising that Perkins remains unwilling to work with Christians who do not agree with him.

A pattern should be evident by now. Christians often seem to compare other Christians to deadly items or animals that are dead or should be dead. As a result, it should not be surprising that these same Christians often seem unable to work with other Christians. Until we begin to view and refer to one another appropriately, there is likely little chance of Jesus' prayer in John 17, that we be united as one, coming true.

The point of this chapter is not that all metaphors are bad but that some of them are. Any metaphor that dehumanizes others and shuts off discussion and cooperation should never be used. Great metaphors are used throughout the Bible and are more appropriate, such as the Body of Christ. This metaphor reminds us that we are all connected and need each other. With this concept in mind, we are not likely to suggest killing the other because that would hurt us. We are more likely to understand the need for us to work together.

Sadly, some of the inappropriate metaphors in Christian discourse use the concept of the body in a negative way. For instance, Southern Baptist Russell Moore called the Cooperative Baptist Fellowship (CBF) "a parasitic movement."[14] Rather than viewing his brothers and sisters as fellow members of the Body of Christ, he sees them as parasites that do not deserve to be there and should be purged. Therefore, it should not be surprising to anyone that Moore frequently attacks CBF as he attempts to hurt its members' ministries.

Other Christians have taken the idea of the Body of Christ and perverted it with metaphors, such as a "cancer lump in the body" that "should be excised,"[15] a "virus,"[16] and a "tumor that

. . . needs to be excised from Christ's body."[17] Each of these
metaphors rejects the opportunity for working together because
one Christian is saying that other Christians should be removed
from the body. Such rhetoric is not only inappropriate; it is
unbiblical. Using this metaphor goes completely counter to
Paul's writings.

Perhaps we should consider again Paul's understanding of
how Christians should relate to and describe each other. In
1 Corinthians 12, Paul writes,

> *Just as a body, though one, has many parts, but all its
> many parts form one body, so it is with Christ. . . . But in
> fact God has placed the parts in the body, every one of
> them, just as he wanted them to be. If they were all one
> part, where would the body be? As it is, there are many
> parts, but one body. The eye cannot say to the hand, "I
> don't need you!" And the head cannot say to the feet, "I
> don't need you!". . . But God has put the body together,
> giving greater honor to the parts that lacked it, so that
> there should be no division in the body, but that its parts
> should have equal concern for each other. If one part suf-
> fers, every part suffers with it; if one part is honored, every
> part rejoices with it. Now you are the body of Christ, and
> each one of you is a part of it.*

Despite this beautiful metaphor that not only allows Christians
to work together—as opposed to the other metaphors examined
here—but also demands cooperation, many seem to say to other
members of the Body of Christ, "I don't need you!" When we do
that either literally or with our metaphors, we are attempting to
break the Body of Christ apart in an unbiblical manner. So be
careful of what metaphors you use. Let us put away the rogue
elephants, dead cats, terrorists, parasites, and cancerous tumors
and focus instead on the Body of Christ.

Notes

[1] Parts of this chapter are drawn from a previous column: Brian Kaylor, "Animals to Kill," BGCM *E-Message*, August 2006, 5.

[2] Tarquin Hall, *To the Elephant Graveyard* (New York: Grove Press, 2000), 7.

[3] George Lakoff and Mark Johnson, *Metaphors We Live By* (Chicago: University of Chicago Press, 1980), 6.

[4] Ibid., 4.

[5] Ibid.

[6] Ibid.

[7] Ibid., 5.

[8] Brian McLaren, "Found in Translation," *Sojourners* 35/3 (March 2006): http://www.sojo.net/index.cfm?action=magazine.article&issue=soj0603&article=060310.

[9] Ibid.

[10] George Lakoff, *Don't Think of an Elephant* (White River Junction VT: Chelsea Green Publishing, 2004), 69.

[11] Louis Sahagun, "Episcopalians Elect Straight Bishop in S.F.," *Los Angeles Times*, 7 May 2006, B1.

[12] Jim Naughton, "Paul Zahl, terrorist," *Daily Episcopalian*, 4 May 2006, http://blog.edow.org/weblog/2006/05/paul_zahl_terrorist.html.

[13] Ibid.

[14] Gregory Tomlin, "CBF church count violates church autonomy, scholars say," *Baptist Press*, 11 August 2006, http://bpnews.net/bpnews.asp?ID=23779.

[15] A response from the House of Bishops of the Church of Nigeria. http://www.anglican-nig.org/response_abc_june06.htm.

[16] Jim Brown, "Horowitz: 'Left-wing virus' rampant on American college campuses," *AgapePress*, 9 January 2003, http://headlines.agapepress.org/archive/1/92003f.asp.

[17] Bill Tully, "What are we, chopped liver?" 31 July 2006, http://www.stbarts.org/blog-post.asp?ID=20.

Chapter 7

Concerned about the Here and Now: The Mistake of Not Speaking at the Appropriate Place and Time

There is a time for everything, and a season for every activity under the heavens: . . . a time to be silent and a time to speak. (Ecclesiastes 3:1, 7b)

Christian comedian and singer Mark Lowry has a song called "First Class, Wrong Flight." In the first verse he sings about how he was running late for his flight to Nashville and barely got on the plane. He then continues the story:

> The flight was overbooked and there was someone in my seat
> So they took me up to first class where they get real food to eat
> I buckled up, we took off, things turned out after all
> 'Til the pilot said "Welcome to our flight to Omaha!"

Sure he was in first class, but he was on the wrong flight and so everything was a mess.

Even though it would be next to impossible for that actually to happen today, many passengers aboard American Airlines Flight 34 on February 6, 2004, must have felt the same way. Shortly after takeoff, pilot Rodger Findiesen came over the intercom and asked those aboard each to raise a hand if they were Christians.[1] He then urged the Christians to spend the long flight from Los Angeles to New York witnessing to those around them. With memories of 9/11 in the air, many passengers began phoning people on the ground warning that a religious zealot was flying the plane. He may not have crashed the plane, but he destroyed his witness.

American Airlines suspended the pilot without pay and apologized for the pilot's behavior. Unfortunately, the damage was done and Christians were mocked and portrayed as religious zealots (and idiots) in the media. What really scared people was that now a traveling evangelist may not be the only person to spiritually accost them on an airplane.

After the flight the pilot explained, "I just wanted to give Christians a chance to talk about why they're Christians."[2] He made the comment in an interview with a journalist who happened to be on the flight and who ironically wrote for *The Advocate*. It was also pointed out that the pilot had just returned from a mission trip to Costa Rica.

It is important to note that this pilot had a good point—Christians need to share their testimony and the "good news" with people around them. Sadly, it is estimated that many if not most Christians have never witnessed to anyone. But regardless of how good your point is, you must also pick the appropriate location and time for saying it. Think about it: you will loudly sing in the shower, but you wouldn't do it in the middle of a crowded mall (maybe, *that's* why people stare at me). Likewise, picking the right place or time to deliver a message is important.

If the Christian pilot (who, when he sings in the shower, perhaps prefers "I'll Fly Away") would have been more careful, he could have aided and not harmed efforts to spread the gospel. He could have spoken at churches, evangelism conferences, or the airport chapel.

Location, Location, Location

Just because you have a good point does not mean you should make it whenever you feel like it. Perhaps one of the ways Christians most often disregard this principle is when they debate with each other in front of non-Christians. Even if your discussion is needed, it's not wise to hang dirty laundry in your neighbor's yard.

I remember one occasion on a long bus trip from the middle of Missouri to New York City with my high school orchestra. Apparently cabin fever got the best of a couple of my Christian friends who decided to engage in a loud and aggressive debate over whether or not Christians should listen to non-Christian music. It's a worthy debate that we should consider as we seek to follow God in all areas of our lives, but they were loud and weren't even sitting next to each other. Instead, between them was a row full of tired and cranky students, mostly nonbelievers. Yet, these students continued. They threw out their verses of support, their arguments questioning each other's claims, and of course their insults. Suddenly other people started talking, but most were taking the opinion of "shut up, you lunatics—I don't care!"

As I watched helplessly from a few rows back, I felt badly for my friends. They were sincerely trying to answer an important question about what it takes to be faithful (you know, the whole "be careful little ears what you hear" thing). But they chose the wrong place to do it (so, "be careful little mouth what you say"). I saw the disgust in the faces of my classmates. My two Christian friends refused to talk to each for a while, but more tragically, both lost credibility in the eyes of many, and their personal witness was weakened.

Real estate experts tell you that when buying, the three most important things to remember are location, location, location. Communicators would be wise to follow such advice. Jesus didn't tell everything to everybody. Many times he took his disciples somewhere away from the crowds to explain a parable or tell them more. If you're having trouble figuring out a safe place for you and your Christian buddy to debate the finer details of faith, ask, "What would Jesus do?" He would probably go up a mountain or into the middle of a lake in a storm.

It's About Time

In London's Hyde Park is an area called Speaker's Corner. For nearly 150 years, people have gone to Speaker's Corner to talk or listen to those who are talking (you can take your picnic lunch, sit back, and enjoy the ramblings of someone who doesn't have a day job). For the most part, the corner has represented the freedom of speech that is so important for democracy, especially for those in the minority. Now Speaker's Corner is the newest target of Christian missionaries.

Jay Smith, a missionary from Pennsylvania, holds weekly seminars for Christians to train them to "go to the Corner for Christ."[3] He's not training them to go and give speeches but to heckle Muslim speakers. Smith was upset by how many Muslims were using Speaker's Corner to try to convert people. So now he trains people to try to out-shout the speakers by quoting controversial verses from the Qur'an.

Do we really want to be known as the best hecklers? Is that going to draw people to Christ? Though a heckler may distract people from being able to hear the speaker, the heckler is also generally not heard. The audience also usually dislikes the heckler due to the person's rudeness and unethical behavior. Smith and his cohorts need to learn to wait until it is their turn to speak (sounds simple enough until you put a dozen preachers in the same room).

To challenge the statements of the Muslim speakers in a loving way in order to persuade people to follow Jesus is not necessarily wrong. I cover the topic of love below, but for those who are impatient, I'll say that I don't think you can consider heckling as a loving act (if you don't believe me, try it on your spouse and see if they feel loved). It is appropriate to try to explain why God is superior to all other gods. After all, the book of Hebrews is basically a well-developed case to prove that Jesus is superior to everyone and everything else in order to urge believers not to return to Judaism.

Smith's problem was not his message as much as it was his poor sense of timing. Comedians will tell you that timing is everything in a joke. He should have trained the other Christians to wait until after the Muslim speaker was done and *then* go up and start talking about Christianity and Jesus. Sometimes it's better to bite your tongue and wait for a better time to speak.

Mark Lowry once sang a comical duet with fellow Christian musician Sandi Patti. The whole song is about him wanting to sing with her, but she rejects him and doesn't want to hurt her career by being in public with him. So they declare that maybe they'll sing together "Another Time, Another Place." Silly and hilarious though he is, Lowry's got good advice for Christians. Sometimes you should wait for another time, another place.

Notes

[1] Maki Becker, "Religious Rant by Pilot's Just Plane Scary," *Daily News* (New York), 8 February 2004, 28.

[2] Derek Rose, "Pilot: On Mission from God," *Daily News* (New York), 11 February 2004, 73.

[3] Sarah Sennott, "Cornered speakers," *Newsweek*, 30 August 2004, 9.

PART II

Becoming a More Effective Communicator

Chapter 8

Practice What You Preach:
Learning More Effective Delivery

But I tell you that people will have to give account on the day of judgment for every empty word they have spoken. For by your words you will be acquitted, and by your words you will be condemned. (Matthew 12:36-37)

There is an epidemic sweeping college campuses today. Blowing through the air, it alarms many students and has created much distress. This menace is none other than sidewalk preachers like the one I mentioned in the introduction. Across the country the preachers may be different, but their message and negative impact on the campuses is quite similar.

While walking quickly to his introduction to public speaking course (to hear an engaging, insightful, and exciting lecture from Professor Kaylor), a student notices a crowd gathered ahead with a loud, booming voice emanating from the center. Without attempting to listen, the student hears the speaker call a couple of passing female students "sluts" and "whores." As the student approaches the building for class, he hears the speaker telling the audience that they are going to hell, and then the door shuts, drowning out the rest of the comments. Such an experience is not rare for the student. Each year the same preacher comes to campus for a few days in early fall or late spring when the weather is nice with the same basic message. It is difficult to avoid campus street preachers because of their loud and theatrical style of speaking and the large crowds that often gather around to gawk or mock.

These preachers argue that only they know God's will and Word. Any student who dares question or challenge them usually is yelled at and condemned to hell. After being accosted on the way to class (sometimes even physically—yes, some of these "preachers" have taken the "Bible thumping" method literally and punched students), many students want to vent and talk about the "crazy" man outside. Such discussions especially come up in a public speaking course. After a couple of semesters, I knew which days students would mention "Brother Jed," whose real name is George Smock.

Eventually I found that I could use "Jed" to teach the students lessons about how *not* to communicate when talking about topics such as ethical communication, logical fallacies, and delivery/style. This chapter is devoted to the latter area. While not all of the items here are something "Jed" necessarily does wrong, each of these can help each of us become better speakers. These lessons are most practical for public speaking, but many of the insights can be used for interpersonal settings as well. The two main areas to examine when attempting to improve one's delivery are voice and body.

Can You Hear Me Now?

Seven points should be considered when attempting to improve the use of your voice. First is pitch, or how high or low you speak. Each of us has a different natural range of pitches in which we speak. The two main things to remember about pitch when you are pitching your ideas are to be natural and to use variety. When we get nervous, we tend to speak at a higher pitch that can be annoying. That is one way people can subconsciously tell when someone is nervous. Relax! Take a deep breath and be yourself. When talking about your faith or sharing your testimony, you do not want to sound like you are making a sales pitch—you want to sound natural. The second aspect of pitch is having variety. We have all suffered (or slept) through the lectures of a monotone professor (which is not me). Since you know how bad it can be, don't do that to people listening to you.

The next important area of vocal delivery is that of rate (i.e., how fast or slowly you speak). If you speak too fast, people may have trouble understanding you or may think you are nervous (or both). If you speak too slowly, people may become bored or think you are dumb (or both). The key is once again to be natural and have variety. Speeding up or slowing down intentionally at times while speaking can help draw attention to what you are saying at that moment and help create emotion.

Closely related to this area is the third aspect of improving the use of one's voice . . . pauses. How often or how long you pause affects your rate. Pauses help you in several ways. First, pauses allow you a moment to stop and think. (Remember, it is always good to think before you speak.) Second, it allows your listeners to digest and think about what you have said so far. If you say something thought provoking, give your audience a second or two to think about it. Otherwise, they will miss the importance of it or think about it and miss what you say next. Furthermore, it can be used to catch your listeners' attention. If you are about to say something important, take a break . . . pause . . . and then say it. Chances are you will recapture their attention before the important statement. Finally, pauses are better than vocal fillers. Usually when we are thinking of our next words, we say "uh," "um," or another annoying filler word. Instead, try to take a silent break and you will appear more polished and intelligent.

The next area of vocal delivery is pronunciation. It is important to try to say your words correctly. If not, you may be judged as not highly intelligent. Whether or not the judgment is accurate, we often judge people's intelligence by how well they speak. Related to this area is the sixth aspect—articulation. While pronunciation is whether you say a word correctly, articulation is how well you say each vowel and consonant sound. It is important to articulate your words well so that people understand what you are saying. The Greek rhetor Demosthenes used to put rocks in his mouth when practicing a speech to help improve his articulation. This is kind of like a baseball player doing a few practice swings with two bats or a track runner practicing with heavier shoes. I'm not advocating that you practice with rocks necessarily—especially if you don't wash them first—but you should attempt to articulate clearly.

Finally, there is the issue of volume—how loudly or softly you speak. With volume there are two things to remember—variety and appropriateness. As far as variety goes, just as it is important not to be monotone, it is important not to be mono-volume. Variety keeps you more exciting as a speaker and can help add emotion or emphasis. When you suddenly get louder or softer, people will pay more attention. A softer volume can evoke a serious or solemn mood, while a louder volume can add excitement. However, it is also important to have an overall appropriate range of volume for your setting. Be too quiet and people won't hear you; be too loud and you will get on people's nerves (especially the ones in their ears). Demosthenes used to practice speaking loudly enough by standing on the beach and speaking into the ocean as the waves crashed in at his feet.

Body of Suggestions

In addition to working on vocal delivery, we also need to work on our body language (and no, I'm not talking about sign language). There are five aspects to consider with the body. While we usually focus on verbal communication, nonverbal communication is also extremely important. The first type of nonverbal communication is personal appearance. This item is a fairly simple one because if you do it right, you don't actually have to think about it while you speak. Whether it is right or not, we judge people based on appearances. While the Christian is not supposed to judge appearances, when talking with others we should dress appropriately for the occasion so that our attire (or lack thereof) does not distract people from what we say.

The second and related area is posture. Again, while this is not an extremely important area, the key is to make sure you do not distract people from what you are saying. The main thing is to act naturally—or maybe just a little better. You do not want to be viewed as fake or odd by adopting an uppity posture, but you also do not want to appear slumped. The next aspect to consider is facial expressions. You want to be sure you complement and not contradict what you say. If you are happy, then your facial expressions should match ("if you're happy and you know it then your face will surely show it"). Likewise, if you are sad or upset, then you should not be smiling (witness those crazy weather guys who interrupt your favorite TV show and smile while they report on severe weather in your area). The other thing to remember is moderation. Don't be distracting because your face is going wild, but also don't be lifeless and show virtually no emotion (i.e., try and find a balance between the Howard Dean scream and the Al Gore drone).

The next component of nonverbal communication to consider is eye contact. This is an important one because it will help you in three ways. First, it says, "I care about you." When we look at people, we show that we want them to hear what we say or we want to hear what they say. It builds rapport, which is a fancy way of saying it helps people to like you. The second advantage of eye contact is that it helps hold people's attention. Without eye contact, people may feel ignored and will be more likely to allow their eyes and minds to wander. Trust me, when I make eye contact with my students they work harder to make sure they appear to be paying attention. Finally, eye contact makes you seem more believable. People who don't look you in the eyes seem untrustworthy or may appear to be hiding something. Eye contact sends the message that you are being open and honest.

The final aspect of body language is gestures. In addition to avoiding certain gestures (you know, the ones you want to use while driving), there are ways we can improve our communication by considering what subtle messages we may be sending through our hands. You do not want to move your hands so much as to be distracting, but you do want to move them some so that you seem alive and animated, which makes you appear more interesting. Moving your hands draws attention to what you are saying at that moment.

George "Jed" Smock violates many of the above principles. His strategy for communicating is to put on a show. He shouts, waves his hands around a lot, and jumps up and down. He will even get right in people's faces to yell and point at them. Students in my public speaking courses overwhelmingly agree that not only is he unethical and illogical, but he is also a poor example of how to communicate. His over-the-top antics reduce him to being merely entertainment. He may get people's attention, but he destroys his credibility and turns them off from his message. At that point he has failed. The real reason to try to improve your delivery is to get your message across. After all, the goal should not be to put on a good show but to lead people to God.

Most of us actually have the opposite problem of Mr. Smock. We often are too laid back, too quiet, or not confident enough to stand up and get people to listen to our message. That is why we must work on being more effective deliverers of the message. We may have the most important thing in the world to say—and I believe as Christians we do—but it will not matter if we cannot get people to listen to us. Please consider these lessons and work to be more effective in your delivery. As I tell my students, if you turn out to be the next "Jed," I will feel that I have failed.

Chapter 9

Talk the Talk:
Keeping a Consistent
and Appropriate Focus[1]

*It is written: "I believed; therefore I have spoken." Since
we have that same spirit of faith, we also believe and
therefore speak, because we know that the one who raised
the Lord Jesus from the dead will also raise us with Jesus
and present us with you to himself. (2 Corinthians 4:13-
14)*

After I preached at a church one Sunday morning, a couple
from the congregation took me out to dinner (those were days
that I, as a poor college student, looked forward to). After our
meal when we got up to pay, the cashier looked upset.
Apparently, the guy who had just paid was quite rude. He had
been upset about something at the restaurant and took it out on
the cashier by yelling and cursing at her. He then left his money
and stormed off. What she said next has stayed with me. She
said, "Maybe at church they should teach him how to treat
people at Sunday dinner."

You've probably heard the statement "You can talk the talk
but can you walk the walk?" It's a good reminder to act and live
like a Christian. However, it makes the incorrect assumption

that most people do actually "talk the talk." Hopefully, by this point you've noticed that Christians often have trouble even with the talking part. The church guy at the restaurant did. If more Christians were able to talk the talk consistently and appropriately, it would make a big difference in our world. Let us learn a few lessons about talking the talk from perhaps the most influential preacher in the modern era—Billy Graham.

When Billy Graham preached his last crusade in June 2005, nearly every newspaper and media outlet in the country—perhaps the world—lavished praise on the man for his nearly half a century of crusades. He has preached to millions of people in more than a hundred countries. Millions have turned their lives over to Jesus as a result of Graham's preaching. During the course of his ministry, many other evangelists have risen and fallen. While we can't all be exactly like Graham, we can learn from him to be more effective in our own lives. Billy Graham is not a bigger Christian; he just had a bigger audience. We can each be a Billy Graham in our own sphere of influence.

Focus

Perhaps the most important lesson each of us can learn from Graham is to focus on the love and grace of God. Throughout the years, Graham's message has remained the same—Jesus loves you, died for you, and will forgive you. Denton Lotz, head of the Baptist World Alliance that unites Baptist bodies around the world (which is a pretty hard task if you think about it), wrote a column honoring Graham and his message. He titled it "Billy Graham's Message: The Same in 1957 and 2005!" Lotz recalled being at the 1957 crusade that Billy Graham held in New York City, the same city where he held his last crusade in 2005. Lotz wrote, "Billy Graham has changed; of course at 86 is older and not the fiery preacher of 1957. But the Gospel Graham preaches never changes. Human methods of proclaiming the Gospel change. Music changes. Church structures change. But, the

Gospel never changes. This message was the same as in 1957."[2] That is a pretty impressive fact when you think about it. The world is not the same, but Graham's message is.

When Graham was preparing to go to New York City in 1957, he wrote in a pamphlet, "The main thrust of the message will be Christ and Him crucified," alluding to Paul's statement in 1 Corinthians 1:23. Throughout Paul's writings you will find him talking about the importance of focusing on Christ and not preaching other or false gospels. He also frequently criticized those whom he felt had gone astray in their message.

Part of maintaining focus on God is to avoid the distractions that creep up along the way. Graham explained why he avoids the distraction of politics (the sirens' call that has shipwrecked many other preachers): "Evangelism is when the gospel, which is good news, is preached or presented to all people. . . . If I took sides in all these different divisive areas, I would cut off a great part of the people that I really want to reach. So I've felt that the Lord would have me just present the Gospel."[3]

Imagine that: a preacher who decided he should just preach! Kind of refreshing, isn't it? Graham knew that *everyone* needs to hear the gospel. Taking sides with a political party or on some other divisive issue can alienate people and keep them from listening to a message about God's love.

While everything you say does not have to be the plan of salvation, all of it should point to—or at least not distract from—God. To talk the talk means keeping a focus on God. As Graham stated on the June 23, 2005, broadcast of CBS's *Today Show*, "I think that if I would talk on a political subject, if I talk about it, it would divide the audience on that issue. That's not my issue. My issue is Christ." Like Paul and Billy Graham, keep your focus on Christ (not the White House, the offering plate, or keeping up with the Joneses).

Positive

Another key lesson we each could learn from Billy Graham is to keep the message positive. If you're like me, you don't like people who are always negative. Likewise, remaining positive as we talk with people is important, especially on spiritual matters. As Dr. Larry Lyon explains about Billy Graham's success, "Here is a man who wasn't damning everyone and everything to hell unless they were exactly like him. . . . Here was a man preaching peace and love in a non-threatening manner that really spoke to a much broader audience."[4] Graham doesn't try to get people to come to God by scaring the hell out of them or hitting them over the head with the Bible or telling them what they can't do. Neither did Jesus. Sometimes I feel that some of these "hellfire and damnation" preachers, like Jonah, actually delight in God's punishment of people.

Perhaps the area in which today's Christians often lose a positive and loving focus is that of homosexuality. Graham explained his thoughts on homosexuals on the June 26, 2005, broadcast of CNN's *Larry King Live*:

> They are created in the image of God, and God loves them. Christ died for them, and he can forgive them of whatever. But you know, we make so much of homosexuality, but it's just one of many sins. There is pride, lust, greed, all these things from [inaudible] through history of people that have lived terrible lives, and those are the things that are the symptoms of a deeper problem.

Here he reiterated God's love for *all* people and went on to list sins that American Christians often commit but ignore. Pointing out the speck in our brother's eye is much easier than dealing with the log in our own. Have you ever seen a fat preacher (and there are plenty of them) preach against gluttony? Have you ever seen an arrogant and money-focused evangelist preach against pride or greed? The key is that regardless of what you've done, God loves you and forgives you. I once saw a *B.C.* cartoon that said the definition of a sermon is something like "An inspiring and powerful message directed to all the people who aren't there." Sadly, that often seems to be true.

If you're wondering what it looks like *not* to follow Billy Graham's example, let me introduce you to a nutcase. In the midst of all the praise for Graham during his last crusade, there were actually a couple of "Christian" leaders who attacked him. During the media coverage surrounding Graham's last crusade, he gave an interview on the *Today Show* with Katie Couric. During the show, he made the comment that he was a lifelong Democrat (but voted based on the candidates rather than solely with his chosen party), but he refused to discuss political or hot-button issues. A number of religious conservatives quickly attacked Graham about his party affiliation.

Reverend Rob Schenck, president of the political activist group the National Clergy Council, stated, "I'm disappointed that my role model of 25 years retained his membership in a party that promotes the expansion of abortion and homosexual marriage. . . . Whoever replaces him will need to hold unequivocal stands on these two paramount moral issues."[5] Billy Graham has helped lead millions of people to God and has inspired millions of others to live their lives more closely to God's Word, and this reverend was upset about a word on Graham's voter registration card. When Jesus came, he cleared the temple of the money changers and said they had turned it into "a den of robbers." Now, I think he would have to throw out all the politicians like the National Clergy Council. I don't think God is going to say to Graham at the pearly gates, "Well, Billy, you did some good stuff for me, but you were a Democrat so I can't let you in. Sorry, but you know I have to have my priorities." Frankly, I suspect that even most atheists would consider Schenck nuts for criticizing Graham.

If this example doesn't convince you of the importance of following Graham's lead in staying focused and positive, then I don't know what will. When Katie Couric asked Graham on the June 23, 2005, broadcast of CBS's *Today Show* what he wanted people to say about him, he stated, "Well, I hope they'll say that he was faithful. That he was faithful to the message all through his life. He didn't depart. He didn't veer. And I'm thankful that I have the help of the Holy Spirit to do that."

Wouldn't it be great if that could be said about each and every Christian? The next time you feel tempted to speak out about some issue, consider first stopping and asking, WWBGS? What would Billy Graham say? He would, like Paul, remain focused on Christ and keep a positive tone. So should each one of us.

Notes

[1] Parts of this chapter are drawn from a previous column: Brian Kaylor, "Lessons from the Life and Ministry of Billy Graham," 20 July 2005, http://www.baptistgcm.org/staff_articles.asp?Staff_ID=1&Article_ID=40.

[2] Denton Lotz, "Billy Graham's Message: The Same in 1957 and 2005!" June 2005, http://bwanet.org/News/05apr-jun/grahammessagesame.htm.

[3] Cathy Lynn Grossman, "The gospel of Billy Graham," *USA Today,* 16 May 2005, 1A.

[4] "A last crusade in a career that reshaped American religion," *Christian Science Monitor,* 24 June 2005, 1.

[5] "Billy Graham a Democrat?" *The Conservative Voice,* 25 June 2005, http://www.theconservativevoice.com/articles/article.html?storyid=6495.

Chapter 10

Fewer Dropped Calls:
Living Up to Our High Calling

As a prisoner for the Lord, then, I urge you to live a life worthy of the calling you have received. (Ephesians 4:1)

During the 2004–05 season of *The West Wing*, the show's characters were in the midst of a presidential election. In one striking episode, the Republican candidate, Arnold Vinick, was repeatedly questioned about why he did not attend church. At one point he was asked whether he would accept an invitation from the Reverend Don Butler, who had run against Vinick in the presidential primaries, to attend Butler's church on the upcoming Sunday. Vinick, played by Alan Alda, responded,

> I respect Reverend Butler. And I respect his church too much to use it for my own political purposes. And that's exactly what I'd be doing if I went down there this Sunday. Because the truth is that it would just be an act of political phonyism. I may be wrong but I suspect our churches already have enough political phonyism.[1]

Now there's a politician I could respect—one who is not willing to (mis)use our churches for political gain. (Plus, Alan Alda just plain looks presidential).

However, in the real world the problem is not only that politicians often take the opposite position as Vinick, but that church leaders gladly welcome them in. Few seem to enjoy playing the game of politics as much as Christians. In the previous chapter, I mentioned Rob Schenck's attack on Billy Graham for being a Democrat. The example of Graham should be enough to prove that one's political affiliation is not as important as his or her church work. (The key to this last statement is "should be," not "is"). Yet, more than ever before, party membership is viewed as a test of religious devotion and faith. Sadly, many Christians have moved their focus so that God's work is overshadowed by that of politicians and lobbyists in Washington, D.C. It is time for Christians to live up to their high calling— one that is much higher than any political office.

Unfortunately, Christians often seem to lose their focus and forsake their true calling to share the love of Jesus with the whole world. In 2004, Republican candidate Alan Keyes attacked his opponent, who is quite religious: "Christ would not vote for Barack Obama."[2] Judy Deats, a Texas Republican, took it a step further as she claimed, "Right now, I wouldn't vote Democratic if Jesus Christ was running."[3] A campaign aide for 2006 Republican candidate Bob Corker in Tennessee—who was running against the religious Harold Ford—said, "To question a Republican's love of God is absolutely over the top and has no place in this campaign."[4] In her 2006 book *Godless: The Church of Liberalism*, pundit Ann Coulter attacked Democrats for being anti-religion and for faking religious faith. However, Coulter apparently is not a member or regular attendee of any church. Perhaps she should offer a disclaimer at every personal appearance: "I'm not a Christian, but I play one on TV, radio, and in books."

Sadly, I could go on with many more examples. Before examining this issue further, however, I should clear up one misconception: I am not a Democrat (I'll wait as shocked readers pick the book back up). The fact is that I often vote for Republicans, though not always. In this chapter, my focus is the misconception that one party is inherently Christian while the other is not. This argument is most often made by Republicans or supporters of the alleged "God's Own Party." Instead of supporting a particular party or candidate, I am more concerned that Christians fulfill their real calling. If we make politics our first love and priority, it will distract us from what really matters.

Inside Politics

Many people have written books over the last couple of years decrying "theocracy" and worrying about the dangers of religion taking over government (a true "theocracy"—or rule by God—is fine with me; it's being ruled by people who think they are God that is more of a concern). However, my concern is not what may be happening to our government, but what is happening to our churches. Compromising and telling the people what they want to hear has become acceptable in the political arena where the focus is to win, but it should not be in churches. All of this became clear to me when I served as a panelist for a public discussion of the documentary *Theologians Under Hitler*. The film, based on a book by Pacific Lutheran University history professor Robert Ericksen, provides a detailed examination of how three prominent theologians used their religious credibility and voice to support Hitler. Watching as German theologians Paul Althaus, Gerhard Kittel, and Emanuel Hirsch moved from preaching the Word of God to proclaiming the gospel of Hitler is chilling. Some argued that Germany was a Christian nation and had God on its side. The Deutsche Christen—or "German Christian"—movement basically contended that the only true Christians were Nazi party members.[5]

My point here is not to compare the situation in America to that of Germany; there are many important differences and I do not want to reduce the horrors of the Holocaust by making such a comparison. What hit me while watching the film was how these brilliant theologians who were doing so much good let politics cut in and interrupt their spiritual race. When churches and Christians become too involved in politics, it is not the government and politicians that suffer most, but the churches and Christians. As former Republican senator and Episcopalian priest John Danforth contended, "When we vest our personal opinions with the trappings of religion, we make religion the servant of our politics. By confusing faith and politics, we become conformed to this world."[6]

When politics becomes a top priority and Christians lose sight of their true calling, then more important work of the church may be pushed aside. Former U.S. senator and presidential candidate Gary Hart, a graduate of Yale Divinity School, argued, "Organized religion that seeks to occupy political power loses its purity and its purpose. Jesus sought to change people's hearts, not their political parties."[7] Hart added, "changing the human heart is the job of religion not the job of politics."[8] Baptist ethicist and *Christianity Today* columnist David P. Gushee has lamented pastors spending their time registering voters instead of "visiting the sick, preaching the gospel, or inviting people to church."[9] Gushee asked, "Is there a direct correlation between our declining confidence in the church and our growing engagement with politics?"[10] It is an excellent question with a disturbing answer. Too often politics seems to be taking away our pure mission, our saltiness.

When churches and religious organizations preach partisan politics, they can be blinded by the errors of those they support (therefore leaving us with the blind leading the blind). The Reverend Jim Wallis has argued,

When either party tries to politicize God, or co-opt religious communities for their political agendas, they make a terrible mistake. The best contribution of religion is precisely not to be ideologically predictable nor loyally partisan. Both parties, and the nation, must let the prophetic voice of religion be heard. Faith must be free to challenge both right and left from a consistent moral ground.[11]

This prophetic voice is desperately needed in our society today, but too many Christians seem more concerned with winning one for "the team." After all, consider how religious conservatives attacked Bill Clinton during the Lewinsky scandal but then made excuses for Tom DeLay and for other Republicans during the Jack Abramoff scandal, or consider the exact opposite responses in both cases by religious liberals.

Primary Colors

In October 2004, Chan Chandler, pastor of East Waynesville Baptist Church in North Carolina, had members who disagreed with his right-wing political views removed from the small congregation. Eventually, amidst the negative press and outcry from concerned Christians, Chandler resigned from the church.[12]

Such a case, sadly, was not the only one in 2004. A church youth group was sent out to find yard signs for Kerry, steal them, and then bring them back to be burned.[13] (Bad pun warning: One would think it would be more biblical to go for burning Bush signs). At a Baptist school, student leaders of the Fellowship of Christian Athletes urged members to vote for Bush and removed a student from leadership for supporting Kerry.[14] Churches, youth groups, and the FCA are supposed to be preaching the love of Jesus, but instead some resort to mere political campaigning. In each of these cases, politics trumped religion.

The biggest problem that can come from a focus on politics is that it cuts us off from reaching people who may have different political beliefs (despite what some may say, people of the other party *are* redeemable). Evangelical megachurch pastor Steve Madsen argued, "Jesus wasn't a Republican or a Democrat . . . I think the church needs to transcend party lines."[15] Madsen added, "If I'm just going to act like a hard-nosed Republican, I'm not going to have credibility with a Democrat . . . And what the church needs is credibility."[16] Evangelical pastor Mark Cox contended, "We vote and we're concerned about issues. But that's not our emphasis. We try to spread the gospel, and tell people about who Jesus Christ is, to trust in God to change hearts—and not worry too much about a political agenda."[17]

Some may argue that preaching the gospel is a political agenda, but that usually comes from people who are preaching politics and trying to act like it is the gospel with selectively chosen proof-texts (also known as taking Scripture out of context and mislabeling it as "preaching").

Megachurch preacher and televangelist Rod Parsley has worked hard to campaign for Republicans and register voters in Ohio. At one political rally that was only thinly veiled as a religious gathering, he called the work a "reformation."[18] Somehow political action has been baptized and sanctified to the point that it is now compared to the work of Martin Luther and others who fought to reform the church and bring the people closer to God. This nonsense from Parsley, whose ministry gives out swords to donors (seriously, I'm not making this stuff up), is laid out in detail in his book *Silent No More* (which is exactly the opposite of how he needs to be acting). Pastor and rhetoric professor Robin Meyers argued that as a result of the mixing of church and state, "Jesus has been silenced by his own church."[19]

Unsaved Democrats listening to Parsley's rhetoric, which is generally filled with war terms, are unlikely to become either Republicans or saved. Though the latter is infinitely more important, I worry that some Christians would be just as concerned about the former (because they believe that "once saved, always Republican"). Conservative Christians Cal Thomas and

Ed Dobson outlined the problems of focusing too much on politics in their book *Blinded by Might*. They argued that politics demands compromise, which is something churches should not do, and that politics is not the most effective way to change the hearts and minds of people. About the political focus of religious groups, they wrote,

> The damage to church is caused by those who appear to the "unchurched" to be interested in ushering in the kingdom of God by force . . . It is transformed from a force not of this world into one that deserves to be treated as just one more competitor for earthly power. It is seen as just another lobbying group to which politicians can toss an occasional bone to ensure loyalty.[20]

With that, the church is co-opted and marginalized (often to the sound of the people saying "amen" and applauding). Because of the warlike nature of politics and the dirty strategies employed, it should not seem surprising that it does not fit well with the mission of churches. This does not mean individual Christians should not be involved in politics. In fact, it would be a serious problem for our nation if none were. However, politics should not become the first priority of churches and religious organizations.

Among the deleted scenes included on the DVD of the 2004 remake of *The Manchurian Candidate*, there is a montage of campaign scenes that did not make it into the movie's final cut. One of the short clips is of a candidate—the Manchurian one—speaking in a church. Unfortunately, similar scenes were not cut from the real campaigns later that year or from the 2006 campaigns. Hopefully in the next election these scenes will be deleted in real life as well.

This coming Sunday I will do something revolutionary—go to church to worship God. I will sing praises to God, not to George Bush or Nancy Pelosi or any other politician. I will listen to the preaching of the gospel of Jesus, not the (false) gospel of

Republicanism or Democratism. I will learn how to live out the teachings of God better, not how to have them codified. After all, Jesus came to build a heavenly kingdom, not an earthly shack. It is time to return to our first love; it is time to live up to our high calling. (I am Brian Kaylor and I approved this message.)

Notes

[1] *The West Wing,* NBC, March 23, 2005.

[2] Cathleen Falsani, "How would Jesus vote?" *Chicago Sun-Times,* 10 September 2004, 32.

[3] "Perspectives," *Newsweek,* 20 March 2006, 25.

[4] Robert Parham, "Democrats narrow 'God gap' in partisan politics," *Knoxville News-Sentinel,* 3 December 2006.

[5] I have written elsewhere about the film: Brian Kaylor, "Heil Hitler," *BGCM E-Message,* February 2006, http://www.baptistgcm.org/staff_articles.asp? Staff_ID=1&Article_ID=65.

[6] John Danforth, *Faith and Politics: How the "Moral Values" Debate Divides America and How to Move Forward Together* (New York: Viking, 2006), 213.

[7] Gary Hart, *God and Caesar in America: An Essay on Religion and Politics* (Golden CO: Fulcrum Publishing, 2005), 34.

[8] Ibid., 55.

[9] David P. Gushee, "Children of a lesser hope," *Christianity Today* 50/11, 94.

[10] Ibid.

[11] Jim Wallis, *God's Politics: Why the Right Gets Wrong and the Left Doesn't Get It* (San Francisco: HarperCollins, 2005), xiv.

[12] Steve DeVane, "Church removes members for political views, deacon says," *The Biblical Recorder,* 9 May 2005, http://www.biblicalrecorder.org/content/news/2005/5_9_2005/ne090505achurch.shtml.

[13] "Pastor apologizes for Kerry sign grab," *Atlanta Journal–Constitution,* 6 November 2004.

[14] Bob Allen, "Student claims dismissal from FCA prompted by vote for Kerry," *Ethics Daily,* 10 December 2004 http://www.ethicsdaily.com/article_detail.cfm?AID=5088.

[15] Matthai Chakko Kuruvila, "Some evangelical Christians reconsider their faith in GOP," *San Francisco Chronicle,* 13 November 2006, A1.

[16] Ibid.

[17] Ibid.

[18] Nate Anderson, "Meet the patriot pastors," *Christianity Today* 50/11, 50.

[19] Robin Meyers, *Why the Christian Right Is Wrong* (San Francisco: Jossey-Bass, 2006), xvii.

[20] Cal Thomas and Ed Dobson, *Blinded by Might* (Grand Rapids: Zondervan Publishing House, 1999), 189.

Chapter 11

The Spiritual Gift of Criticism: Giving and Receiving Criticism

Preach the word; be prepared in season and out of season; correct, rebuke and encourage—with great patience and careful instruction. (2 Timothy 4:2)

If you haven't noticed by now, I feel constructive criticism is a necessity. Some may say I'm too harsh and that we should not judge or criticize others (which would, ironically, be criticizing me), but remember that Paul did it. And Paul didn't criticize just anybody—he took on Peter himself. If you're not familiar with the story, check it out in Galatians. In today's reading of the early church, we often view Paul as the top dog since he wrote so much of the New Testament (though John and Luke actually wrote more words than Paul). But Peter was also big, if not bigger, in the early church. After all, Paul had been the persecutor, but Peter was one of the disciples and the preacher at the Day of Pentecost. For anyone to challenge Peter would be like someone today taking on Billy Graham or some other prominent preacher.

I firmly believe criticizing fellow Christians is not only okay, but can even be our duty. If someone has gone astray or is hurting the image of Christians—and thus Christ—then someone desperately needs to step in and try to fix the problem or at least stop the bleeding. Just because you criticize someone does not mean that you do not like them or respect them. In fact, I still have great respect for several of the Christians leaders whom I have used as examples thus far. That's why I truly hope they will not hurt their credibility or ministry by saying harmful things.

For instance, earlier I commented on something Dr. James Dobson said at Justice Sunday. However, I think Dobson has done *great* things for Christian families. My wife and I were both reared by parents who read and implemented Dobson's ideas (at least she turned out perfect; but don't blame Dobson or my parents for my failures). I still think Dobson is a great family counselor, just an awful politician. I would hate to see him say things now that undermine his years of ministry.

In case you're still skeptical, let me turn to Cal Thomas, a conservative commentator and former leader of the Moral Majority. Thomas coauthored a book criticizing the over-politicizing of the church of which he used to be a part. One chapter he wrote focuses on Dobson. It is appropriately called "Focus on the Family, Not on Politics." After criticizing Dobson for several pages, Thomas wrote,

> Our response to Dr. Dobson's political activism has been strong and emphatic. We believe that he and his organization, Focus on the Family, have done more than anyone else or any other organization to strengthen the family in our nation. It is our concern that his current focus on politics will derail and dilute the good he is doing through Focus on the Family. Furthermore, we fear that this focus on politics will help to obscure the central message of the gospel, which is about personal, not political, redemption.[1]

Thomas also wrote that after he criticized Dobson one time, Dobson returned fire and criticized him back. Thomas then added, "That's okay—I can dish it out, and I can take it, too."[2] That's a good reminder because criticism cuts both ways. We are all human, and we will all make mistakes. Each of us has surely said something we wish we could take back. Thus, we must look at how to give and receive criticism appropriately. Hopefully through this process we will be able to improve the image of Christianity and become more effective in sharing our beliefs.

Better to Give than to Receive

While I believe helping others realize when they are unintentionally hurting the cause and then helping them remedy the situation is important, the process is also delicate and should not be taken lightly. Here are a few things to remember as you consider whether to criticize someone and how. The first and most important consideration is to be positive. At first, positive criticism may sound like an oxymoron. However, there are different ways to criticize someone. The key to effective criticism is to offer the person you are addressing some way to remedy the situation. Don't just attack them; instead, provide reasoning to support your point and then offer a positive suggestion on a better way to communicate. Don't call them names or aggressively attack them. Simply point out the problem and what needs to be done differently without resorting to rudeness and insults.

Next, have a beneficial purpose. You should not attack someone just because you want to. You should only criticize someone in order to make things better, not merely to rub salt in their wounds. For me, this is the most important question to ask: will what I'm about to say or write help the kingdom? If not, I try to bite my tongue (or hand) and keep it to myself.

For instance, when Jerry Vines made his comment about Muhammad at a meeting in St. Louis (see chapter 2), I was there. I got the newspaper the next day as usual. I found that Christians were getting pretty beat up because of it. I decided that someone needed to put in a good word for us, and I wrote a letter to the editor that was published in the *St. Louis*

Post-Dispatch. While it criticized Vines, my primary purpose was to help reduce the damage being done to the Christian image. While it is probably not perfect (in my defense, I was a young foolish college student at the time), here it is:

> As a Southern Baptist who was present when Rev. Jerry Vines made his comments about Islam, I must express my regret and outrage at his statements. Do not read them to be representative of all Southern Baptists. Though I may agree with his premise (that God and Allah are not the same), I take issue with his expression of it. We must enter into dialogue and not resort to stereotyping and polarizing comments. Most Southern Baptists reach out to those of different faiths in love, not hate. Hopefully, our leaders will someday preach what we practice.[3]

My purpose in writing this book is much the same—I desperately hope and pray that Christians will improve their communication for God's sake.

Another important piece of advice about offering criticism of someone else is to remember the other lessons already covered in this book. Like any form of communication, criticism should follow these basic ideas. Here's a quick review: First, carefully listen to the person to make sure you hear them correctly and truly understand what they are saying. Second, choose your battles carefully—if your criticism will not help the kingdom, then don't give it. Next, consider the consequences of your words to make sure they will not make the situation worse. Fourth, avoid logical fallacies. Next, make sure you pick the appropriate time and place to offer the criticism. Sixth, practice it to make sure it is well put. Finally, remain focused and positive.

You've probably heard that "it is better to give than to receive." While I've never been convinced about the accuracy of that saying, criticism is one area where it is true. Thus, be willing to offer constructive criticism in order to help your fellow

Christians. But it is also important to know how to react when *you* are criticized, because it will probably happen.

The Gift that Keeps on Giving

At some point you will probably be criticized, and you may deserve it. Here's some advice on how to accept and evaluate criticism in order to improve your own communication. First, don't react defensively, even though that is a natural reaction. This is especially important if you are receiving criticism personally from someone and not in writing. Let the other person speak their mind, listen to them, and consider their thoughts. In the "Old West," if someone criticized you, then you would generally challenge them to a duel. Such a response accomplished little (except population control), and it won't help you either. If you can find it within yourself, try to thank the person who has offered the criticism.

Next, try honestly and carefully to consider the comments to determine if there is any merit to the criticism. Usually there is at least some truth in the criticism, even if parts are inaccurate. Thus, you need to learn how to pick out the good comments that can be helpful to you. Finally, try to remember the wisdom you've gleaned from the criticism and avoid making the same mistakes in the future.

Criticism. It is an ugly word in our society, but it can be a good thing as we try to hold each other accountable and work together to tell the world about God. The worst thing would be for Christians to ignore each other's faults and never try to help each other improve. While Paul did not include criticism in the list of spiritual gifts, it can still be an important service to perform. Maybe together we can finally figure out how best to communicate and represent God.

Notes

[1] Cal Thomas and Ed Dobson, *Blinded by Might* (Grand Rapids: Zondervan Publishing House, 1999), 126-27.

[2] Ibid., 119.

[3] Brian Kaylor, letter to the editor, *St. Louis Post-Dispatch*, 18 June 2002, B6.

Chapter 12

By Invitation Only: How to Measure Success Appropriately

You must speak my words to them, whether they listen or fail to listen. (Ezekiel 2:7a)

While I was in high school I volunteered for several political campaigns, most of which resulted in losses. However, one state senate candidate I worked for, along with some of my friends, actually did win. Because of my work as the organizer of high school volunteers, I was given an invitation to the governor's inaugural ball. I was ecstatic! That invitation is still by far the fanciest I have ever received. At the event, I was surrounded by free food and drinks, politicians, and about three lobbyists for every person there. Even though I knew virtually no one at the party, I enjoyed myself.

Unfortunately, such a closed by-invitation-only atmosphere is not only found at political events or weddings (I do not wish to imply any other similarities between the two). Churches are also accused of having a select membership kind of like a country club. A Florida pastor talked to a local newspaper reporter about how his church was planning a new and attractive building. He then added, "A church is like a country club. It has to attract people, and among the things that help do that is the look of the building."[1] Such a comment likely drives away poor and middle-class people who do not want yet another institution where they can be looked down upon or excluded.

Invitation Time

Fortunately, even though they might not actually do it, most Christians seem to believe we should work to bring more people to church so they, too, can discover the love of Jesus. When we do get out there to witness to people, though, we often get focused on the numbers: how many did you win? Yet, our job is not to reach some quota of converts each year. Our job is to tell. Our job is not to win people for God but to invite them to accept God's love.

Don't misunderstand me. I am not putting down those who see large numbers of people make decisions. But that is not how spiritual success is measured. In our society, success is always quantified, whether it be sports stats, test scores, job performance levels, etc. But our job is to tell it the best way we possibly can.

If someone does not come to Christ after talking with us, that does not mean we failed. As long as we planted a seed and did not push them further away from God, we did our part for now. Before becoming a Christian, the average person hears the gospel 7.6 times.[2] You never know. Yours may be the first, second, or sixth seed being planted. Thus, it does not matter how many people you have talked to that have actually accepted Christ, but how many you have invited to do so.

In the field of academic communication studies, there is a theory that I believe captures this appropriate perspective for how a Christian should measure success—invitational rhetoric. Scholars Sondra Foss and Cindy Griffin explain that this type of rhetoric "is an invitation to understanding as a means to create a relationship."[3] With this relationship focus, people are no longer reduced to conversion numbers but are viewed as people. This rhetoric is not an attempt at persuasion per se, but rather "an invitation to the audience to enter the rhetor's world and to see it as the rhetor does."[4] You simply want them to understand what God has done and means to you. If they truly understand that, then they will likely feel the Spirit knocking on their hearts (which is much more effective than you knocking them down with an aggressive tone or angry words).

Under this perspective you do not criticize the person for not suddenly repenting. That is an issue between them and God (and you are not God). This invitational style of communication can help "create an environment that facilitates understanding, accords value and respect to others' perspectives, and contributes to the development of relationships of equality."[5] In other words, this type of communication opens doors and invites people in for a cup of coffee. As the slogan for the United Methodist Church wisely puts it, "Open Hearts, Open Minds, Open Doors."

I believe this is the type of rhetoric Jesus engaged in as he invited people into the kingdom of God. His words were designed to build bridges for people, not cut them off. Brian McLaren put it well in a *Sojourners* column as he talked about the communication style of Jesus.[6] He offered several pieces of advice drawn from the example of Jesus to help Christians become bridge builders. He urged us to avoid bad or trick questions that can turn the conversation into a confrontational one; start asking more questions to get people to think; dig deeper than we often go in our trite and polarized discussions; speak with words and actions; tell more stories; and agree as often as we can with people.

This invitational style of communication will build bridges, open doors, and help people to understand our thoughts about God. An ad for the United Church of Christ showed bouncers turning people away from church and then had this text: "Jesus didn't turn people away. Neither do we." Hopefully that can be said someday of all churches and Christians. If we do the inviting well, then we can turn the rest of the work over to God (and trust me, God is so much better at winning people than we are).

Watch Your Mouth![7]

I used to make smart-aleck remarks when I was younger and less mature. Sometimes after I made a sarcastic comment, my mom would tell me to "watch my mouth," to which I would respond by sticking my lips out as far as I could and try to look down and see them. That, of course, was not what she meant—she wanted me to be careful about what I say. With her meaning in mind, I offer the following advice—watch your mouth!

Unfortunately, such advice does need to be given to many people in our society. We seem to be more polarized and aggressive in our rhetoric in recent years. Attorney Gerald Skoning argued,

> There's an old trial lawyers' adage about how to argue a case: "If you have the facts, argue the facts. If you have the law, argue the law. And if you don't have either, shout a lot." . . . The decibel level has risen to intolerable levels. The fine art of civil discourse is being drowned out under ear-piercing invective.[8]

Columnist John Leo wrote, "We have reached the point where much political debate consists of insults and name-calling. . . . So political discussion more and more consists of angry feelings instead of rational argument."[9]

Sadly, Christians often adopt this overly aggressive tone. Much of the problem seems to stem from the desire to beat the other person (literally or otherwise). However, if we would recognize that our job is to invite and not persuade, such a tone would be seen as unnecessary.

A common way this aggressive tone is used is when derogatory adjectives are added before the name of an individual or organization to attack them. Such name-calling is not only inaccurate, but it only makes the situation worse. While we may expect this type of mudslinging in politics, it should have no place in church life. Jesus told us, "Let your 'yes' be 'yes' and your 'no' be 'no.'" Likewise, it is sometimes best to let your nouns be nouns without any adjectival garnish.

The worst comments I have seen are those that compare Christian or other political leaders to Adolf Hitler or the Nazis. For instance, Don Hinkle, editor of the Missouri Baptist Convention's (MBC) publication *The Pathway*, attacked the leaders of the Baptist ministry organizations who were attempting to clear their name in the midst of an MBC lawsuit against them. He wrote, "This massive outpouring of publicity that would have impressed Joseph Goebbels for its breadth and ferocity, has gotten them little to nothing."[10] He compares his brothers and sisters in Christ, who are working to share the love of Jesus, to a man who was one of Hitler's main leaders and morally responsible for the deaths of millions of people. Comments such as this demonstrate that the speaker is so hell-bent on winning that he or she would say just about anything.

The Holocaust resulted in ethnic genocide that killed ten million people, and World War II led to the deaths of more than fifty million people. No matter how much you disagree with a nonviolent person, they have not done anything even remotely close to the atrocities committed by the Nazi regime. Such Hitler or Nazi rhetoric is completely out of line, inaccurate, and un-Christlike. As Kathleen Parker put it,

> This compulsion to Hitlerize our political foes, though their deeds justify no such moniker, trivializes one of history's true monsters. This tendency to Nazi-fy any unwelcome action, though it falls far short of the atrocities committed by real Nazis, cheapens the horror of historical events. . . . What's clear is that playing the Hitler card is a cheap trick designed only to sensationalize and stir emotions.[11]

As Jon Stewart so wisely put it on the June 16, 2005, broadcast of *The Daily Show*, "You know who was Hitler? Hitler."

When I was being a sarcastic teenager, my mother would sometimes say, "Don't take that tone with me!" As we share our beliefs, we must be careful of what tone we are taking. We do not want to become so focused on winning an argument that we end up losing overall by driving someone away from God. Therefore, watch your mouth!

Winning is nice and we humans seem to like it. But when it comes to sharing the love of Jesus, winning is not the focus. Witnessing is not a game, and even if it were, it is not ours to win. Therefore, I wish we would quit talking about us "winning" people to Christ because the only one who won anything for anybody was the One who died on the cross! We can tell, invite, and maybe even lead, but not win.

Do not misunderstand me. I am not saying we should not try to witness to people. Rather, I'm saying we *must* tell people about the love of Jesus, but in a different way. Just because we are not persuading them does not mean we are not telling. We must take every opportunity to invite people to the King's banquet (see Luke 14).

We should measure success not by how many notches we have in our (Bible) belts, but how many people with whom we were able to share and dialogue. We should only use invitational rhetoric, but we need to send out as many invitations as we possibly can. "By Invitation Only" is not a good way for a congregation to operate, but it is exactly how our communication should work.

Notes

[1] K. Partington, "Bonita advisory committee seeks advice on whether churches can be included in architectural reviews," *Bonita Banner,* 27 September 2003, www.bonitanews.com.

[2] William Fay and Linda Shepherd, *Share Jesus without Fear* (Nashville: Broadman & Homan, 1999), 11.

[3] Sonja K. Foss and Cindy L. Griffin, "Beyond Persuasion: A Proposal for an Invitational Rhetoric," *Communication Monograph* 62/1 (March 1995): 5.

[4] Ibid.

[5] Ibid., 17.

[6] Brian McLaren, "A Bridge Far Enough?: How would Jesus address the issues of our day?" *Sojourners* 34/9 (September/October 2005): http://www.sojo.net/index.cfm?action=magazine.article&issue=soj0509&article=050910.

[7] Parts of this section are drawn from a previous column: Brian Kaylor, "Watch Your Mouth!" 28 September 2005, http://www.baptistgcm.org/staff_articles.asp?Staff_ID=1&Article_ID=57.

[8] Gerald D. Skoning, "Turning down the volume," *Chicago Tribune,* 11 November 2004, 17.

[9] John Leo, "The End of Argument," *U.S. News & World Report* 138/15 (25 April 2005): 67.

[10] Don Hinkle, "Sooner or later, the 'Rebel Five's' spin machine will blow an engine," *Pathway,* 30 March 2004, http://www.mbcpathway.com/hinklecolumns/article-1999942729.htm.

[11] Kathleen Parker, "Go ahead and make your point, but leave Hitler out of it," *Kansas City Star,* 25 October 2005, B5.

Chapter 13

What's Love Got to Do With It?
—Everything!

If we say we love God yet hate a brother or sister, we are liars. (1 John 4:20a)

The city of Dover, Pennsylvania, still stands. Following the rout of eight school board members who had voted to include the teaching of intelligent design, televangelist Pat Robertson announced (almost with a mafia-like wink) that Dover would be "in trouble." He added that they had better not expect God to come to their aid. Robertson declared that Dover had "voted God out" (though I am not sure which of the eight candidates he was referring to as God). He then added advice that seemed to represent the exact opposite of a traditional preacher's message: "don't turn to God."

As with most of Robertson's "prophesies," nothing seems to have happened. Maybe this one belongs in the unfulfilled pile along with his statements that God told him he would win the presidency in 1988.

The Dover warning came less than two months after Robertson issued a religious fatwa against Venezuelan president Hugo Chavez. Robertson once again seemed to speak as God's hit man. Robertson would return to this message of hate and death two months after the Dover remarks as he declared that Israeli prime minister Ariel Sharon's stroke was part of "God's wrath" for removing Israeli settlements. As with the Chavez statement, Robertson would eventually apologize for this one, which suggests it really was not God's message.

Before the Sharon apology, Robertson's spokeswoman, Angell Watts, defended him by attacking his critics: "What they're basically saying is, 'How dare Pat Robertson quote the Bible?' This is what the word of God says." I missed the verse warning Sharon that if he took down the settlements he would have a stroke. Robertson can quote Scripture until he is blue in the face, but it will do no good unless he has love.

As Paul so eloquently put it in 1 Corinthian 13,

If I speak in human or angelic tongues, but do not have love, I am only a resounding gong or a clanging cymbal. If I have the gift of prophecy and can fathom all mysteries and all knowledge, and if I have a faith that can move mountains, but do not have love, I am nothing. If I give all I possess to the poor and give over my body [to hard-ship] that I may boast, but do not have love, I gain nothing.

Robertson can speak, prophesy, or give to the poor all day, but it is nothing without love. Out of all the problems with Christian communication identified in this book, the lack of love guiding our words may be the greatest problem. Maybe the problem isn't with Robertson's mouth, but his heart. Unfortunately, he is not the only clanging cymbal out there claiming to speak for God.

Blowing Hot Air

In August 2005, the United States was hit with one of its worst natural disasters as Hurricane Katrina flooded the city of New Orleans and devastated much of the gulf coast region. Many Christian denominations and organizations responded with

Christlike love by quickly sending donations and teams to help bring much-needed relief to the area. Without saying a word, a powerful message of love was delivered. Unfortunately, some Christian leaders decided instead to open their mouths and offer words of hate and condemnation.

Reverend Rick Scarborough suggested America deserved the hurricane because of support for homosexual marriage, pornography, problems in public schools, and the removal of the Ten Commandments. He declared, "We are sowing the wind. Surely, we shall reap the whirlwind."[1] However, a year before the hurricane, Louisiana voters overwhelmingly approved a constitutional amendment banning same-sex marriage (apparently God has not kept up with the news).

Scarborough also linked the Gaza withdrawal to Hurricane Katrina. He argued, "One other factor which must be considered: Days before Katrina nearly wiped New Orleans off the map, 9,000 Jewish residents of Gaza were driven from their homes with the full support of the United States government."[2]

Bill Shanks, pastor of New Covenant Fellowship of New Orleans, also thanked God for Hurricane Katrina. He declared, "New Orleans now is abortion free. New Orleans now is Mardi Gras free. New Orleans now is free of Southern Decadence and the sodomites, the witchcraft workers, false religion—it's free of all of those things now."[3] It was also free of living people. How could someone be so heartless? This rich white pastor who fled the city and condemned the poor black people left behind to die doesn't sound like the "the good Samaritan".

In Luke 19:41 Jesus wept—not thanked God—over the city of Jerusalem because of the coming destruction. Our loving Jesus probably wept over the city of New Orleans as well (and the comment of Shanks). How does this New Orleans "preacher" ever expect to reach people after praising God for a disaster that killed so many? What's even more interesting is that his church was badly damaged by the hurricane. Using Shank's logic, it must have been God's punishment.

Several other religious leaders made similar comments. The leader of an anti-homosexual group, Repent America, said the hurricane was God's punishment for homosexuality. Shortly thereafter, an editorial cartoon showed God on the telephone saying, "Hello? Repent America? God here. Listen, thanks for the free publicity and all, but do me a favor and DON'T do me any favors, okay?" It would be funnier if it weren't so true.

In the wake of disasters, many Christians quickly respond and live out the teachings of Jesus. In fact, if we would act like that all of the time, I bet we would see many more people respond to the gospel. When I see this positive and helpful reaction, I am never more proud to be called a Christian. However, when some hateful individuals claiming to be "preachers" rhetorically kick people while they are down and blaspheme God with their judgmental pronouncements, I am never more ashamed to be called a Christian.

Sometimes the best thing we can do is to keep our mouths shut and show people the love of Jesus. Anyone who revels in the pain and suffering of others cannot possibly speak for God. As we are reminded in 1 John 4:7-8, "Dear friends, let us love one another, for love comes from God. Everyone who loves has been born of God and knows God. Whoever does not love does not know God, because God is love."

When Pat Robertson linked Hurricane Katrina to abortion, he referred to an Old Testament passage, but maybe if he read the 1 John passage we might get a different message. Either way, it would be great if next time the only response to a natural disaster is the loving relief, and the only harmful hot air blowing in is that from the actual storm.

City of Brotherly Hate

On October 11, 2004, eleven members of Repent America (RA) were arrested while protesting at OutFest, an annual homosexual rally in Philadelphia. Four of the demonstrators were charged with several crimes that could have sentenced them to up to forty-seven years in prison, and a teenager faced charges in the juvenile justice system.

The group claims they only preach in love (apparently with the same love that led the group's leader to say that New Orleans deserved Hurricane Katrina because of its acceptance of homosexuality). The group was holding signs and reading passages from the Bible with bullhorns about homosexuals burning in hell.

Franny Price, executive director of the group that organizes OutFest, stated, "Jesus doesn't come in there with a bullhorn."[4] It is pretty sad when the OutFest organizer seems to understand Jesus better than some Christian "preachers" (then again, common fishermen understood Jesus better than the hateful Pharisees and teachers of the law).

Christian groups and leaders were quick to declare their outrage that these individuals were arrested for preaching from the Bible (though not apparently from any of the Gospels). The charges were eventually dropped, but RA sued the city of Philadelphia over the incident.

The rhetoric surrounding this case was intense, but no one seemed to ask whether the protesters should have acted or spoken that way in the first place. Just because one has the right to say something does not mean it is right to say it. Repent America tries to justify what they do by quoting Scripture, but for every verse they quote condemning homosexuality, I can give them a dozen about God's love.

Even though the charges against them were dropped, these protestors have hurt the kingdom and likely driven many people away from God's love and saving grace. One "preacher" with his "God Abhors You" sign stated in an interview, "At this point, you're not going to get converts. This is their big day. But I'm here to rain on their parade."[5] He admits his actions will not bring anyone to God but that he wants to make them mad. So much for Christian love (or intelligence)!

Maybe RA and other Christians should try being more Christlike in their comments. After all, Jesus spent his time talking about love and the kingdom, not about how homosexuals will burn in hell. The homosexual community knows what the Bible says and what evangelicals think about homosexuality. However, what they do not know is what the Bible says about the love of Jesus (it is sad that more protesters carry signs quoting Leviticus 18:22 than John 3:16).

The protesters were right when they insisted that we need to speak to the homosexual community, but they chose the wrong message, and thus they were wrong in what they did. Philadelphia used to be called the "City of Brotherly Love" because of the Christians who founded it and lived there. Now a few Philadelphia believers are turning Christianity into a religion of hate and fear. As one Pennsylvania legislator declared after the RA arrests, "Philadelphia is a national embarrassment."[6] Sadly, Christians have made it so.

When he was arrested, RA leader Michael Marcavage was photographed flipping through a hymnal. Maybe he should have checked out the classic hymn that reminds us to tell the story of God's love: "I love to tell the story of unseen things above, of Jesus and His glory, of Jesus and His love."

In 1984, Tina Turner topped the charts with her song asking, "What's love got to do with it?" For the Christian the answer is everything! Every word from our mouths, every thought we have, and everything we do must be done in love.

Notes

[1] Rick Scarborough, "New Orleans - When God Opens the Floodgates," *The Rick Scarborough Report*, 2 September 2005, http://www.visionamerica.us/site/DocServer/rsr0124.pdf?docID=212..

[2] Ibid.

[3] Jody Brown and Allie Martin, "New Orleans Residents: God's Mercy Evident in Katrina's Wake," *AgapePress*, 2 September 2005, http://headlines.agapepress.org/archive/9/2005b.asp..

[4] Bill Toland, "In-Your-Face Evangelist Tests Hate-Crime Law Limits," *Pittsburgh Post-Gazette*, 23 January 2005, A14.

[5] Natalie Pompilio, "Gay pride celebrated with little disruption," *Philadelphia Inquirer,* 10 October 2005, http://www.philly.com/mld/inquirer/12862133.htm.

[6] Bill Toland, "Hate Crimes Change Sought," *Pittsburgh Post-Gazette*, 8 February 2005, A8.

(I Get the Last Word!)

Each year since 1990, the American Dialect Society (doesn't that sound like a fun group) selects a word of the year. Founded in 1889 to study the English language and its evolution (I mean, its intelligent design), the ADS is made up of linguists, lexicographers, etymologists, historians, grammarians, academics, editors, and writers. The words or phrases are chosen as the ones that best capture the news of the year. The winning entries are often words that suddenly become used often or are even made up during the year (it is kind of like the Oscars for word geeks).

For 2005, the ADS chose "truthiness" as the word of the year. Unless you watch *The Colbert Report* on Comedy Central, you probably have not heard this word, since comedian Stephen Colbert introduced it in a daily segment he calls "The Word." Truthiness is defined by the society as "the quality of stating concepts or facts one wishes or believes to be true, rather than concepts or facts known to be true." As Colbert explained, "I don't trust books. They're all fact, no heart." In hopes of making the ADS list, I am hereby making up the following word—communikaze, or someone who kills their cause by what they say.

Other top words included "intelligent design," "refugee," and "heck of a job"—a phrase coined by President George W. Bush in describing the work of failed FEMA chief Michael

Brown. The ADS also selected top words for 2005 in other categories, such as Most Useful ("podcast"), Most Unnecessary ("K Fed" for Kevin Federline, the ex-Mr. Britney Spears), Best Tom Cruise-Related Word ("jump the couch"), Most Likely to Succeed ("sudoku," a Japanese number puzzle game), and Least Likely to Succeed ("pope-squatting," which involved the registering of Internet domain names of potential popes before the conclave election).

Looking back on previous winners reminds us of what our society was talking about in those years, like taking a linguistic trip into the past. Previous words of the year included "red/blue/purple states" (2004), "weapons of mass destruction" (2002), "chad" (2000), "Y2K" (1999), "World Wide Web" (1995), and "not!" (1992). Previous winners in other categories have included "blog" (Most Likely to Succeed, 2002), "google" (Most Useful, 2002), "Let's Roll!" (Most Inspirational, 2001), "senior moment" (Most Euphemistic, 1998), "go postal" (Most Original, 1995), "McJob" (Most Imaginative, 1993), and "politically correct" (Most Outrageous, 1990).

Words are important. The words we choose can tell others a lot about what we believe. Choosing one word over another may seem like a simple matter of preference, but it actually can give a glimpse into one's background and worldview. For instance, whether one says "soda," "pop," or "coke" offers insights into the person's background. On a more important level, corporations and organizations spend immense amounts of time and energy writing mission and purpose statements. They often debate over the nuances of various words to find the one that best communicates the intended message.

Author Oliver Wendell Holmes argued, "Speak clearly, if you speak at all; carve every word before you let it fall." Humorist Mark Twain explained, "The difference between the right word and the almost right word is the difference between lightning and a lightning bug." Clearly, carefully choosing the words one uses is important. As pastor Joel Osteen stated, "You can change your world by changing your words . . . Remember, death and life are in the power of the tongue."

My earnest prayer with this book is that Christians would begin to find the right words to say in the right way in order to lead people to God. Much of this book has been devoted to showing examples of common blunders Christians make and how in those cases it would have been better if they had kept their mouths shut. As Paul wrote in Titus 1:10-11, "For there are many rebellious people, full of meaningless talk and deception . . . They must be silenced, because they are disrupting whole households by teaching things they ought not to teach—and that for the sake of dishonest gain." Sounds like there was some truthiness going on!

My real goal is not to silence Christians—just the junk that may come from their mouths. In reality, I hope that by my pointing out these failures, you can now more effectively communicate your beliefs. The world desperately needs to hear about the love of Jesus. Once we learn how to avoid driving people away, we must, for God's sake, speak up! Please try to remember these lessons, and then get out there and tell people. Words. Our language is always changing, and there is always more to learn (including new words like "truthiness" and "communikaze"). Likewise, we always have more to learn about being effective communicators. Christians—myself included—still have much to learn. But that is part of what it means to be a disciple, or follower, of Jesus. We should always be growing and improving. As religion professor Rodney Reeves explained,

> We shouldn't believe that we're uniquely qualified to wield the sword of Christ's kingdom with powerful words. . . . Sometimes we speak the truth when all else are silent. But most of the time, we don't understand and we don't know what to do. Talk less, listen more. Jesus is the beloved Son of God, God's choice servant—no one else. Those who are kept closest to his side need the most help. Sometimes I wish I could learn to keep my mouth shut.[1]

If only all of us were as deliberate about trying to become better disciples and ambassadors.

Hopefully this is not the last word, but just the beginning of a much-needed discussion and dialogue in the Christian community. I do not have all of the answers (probably not even as many as I think I do), but I do know that we need to continue to "spur one another on toward love and good deeds" (Hebrews 10:24). Please continue thinking, reading, and discussing how we can be effective spokespeople for God with our mouths.

And let's continue the dialogue. Join me at my blog www.forgodssakeshutup.blogspot.com and we can continue to discuss these important issues. Maybe together we can help rid the Christian community of communikazes. As Stephen Colbert states, "And that's the word." But hopefully not the last one.

Note

[1] Rodney Reeves, *A Genuine Faith* (Grand Rapids: Baker Books, 2005), 51.

Other available titles from SMYTH& HELWYS®

#Connect
Reaching Youth Across the Digital Divide
Brian Foreman

Reaching our youth across the digital divide is a struggle for parents, ministers, and other adults who work with Generation Z—today's teenagers. *#Connect* leads readers into the technological landscape, encourages conversations with teenagers, and reminds us all to be the presence of Christ in every facet of our lives.   *978-1-57312-693-9 120 pages/pb* **$13.00**

Atonement in the Apocalypse
An Exposé of the Defeat of Evil
Robert W. Canoy

Revelation calls believers to see themselves through the unique lens of redemptive atonement and to live and model daily that they see themselves in the present moment as redeemed people. Having thus seen themselves, believers likewise are directed to see and to relate to others in this world the very way that God has seen them from eternity.   *978-1-57312-946-6 218 pages/pb* **$22.00**

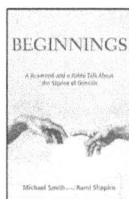

Beginnings
A Reverend and a Rabbi Talk About the Stories of Genesis
Michael Smith and Rami Shapiro

Editor Aaron Herschel Shapiro declares that stories "must be retold—not just repeated, but reinvented, reimagined, and reexperienced" to remain vital in the world. Mike and Rami continue their conversations from the *Mount and Mountain* books, exploring the places where their traditions intersect and diverge, listening to each other as they respond to the stories of Genesis.   *978-1-57312-772-1 202 pages/pb* **$18.00**

Bugles in the Afternoon
Dealing with Discouragement and Disillusionment in Ministry
Judson Edwards

In *Bugles in the Afternoon*, Edwards writes, "My long experience in the church has convinced me that most ministers—both professional and lay—spend time under the juniper tree. Those ministers who have served more than ten years and not been depressed, discouraged, or disillusioned can hold their annual convention in a phone booth."

    978-1-57312-865-0 148 pages/pb **$16.00**

To order call **1-800-747-3016** or visit **www.helwys.com**

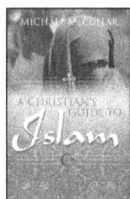

A Christian's Guide to Islam
Michael D. McCullar

A *Christian's Guide to Islam* provides a brief but accurate guide to Muslim formation, history, structure, beliefs, practices, and goals. It explores to what degree the tenets of Islam have been misinterpreted, corrupted, or abused over the centuries.

978-1-57312-512-3 128 pages/pb **$16.00**

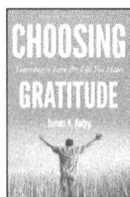

Choosing Gratitude
Learning to Love the Life You Have

James A. Autry

Autry reminds us that gratitude is a choice, a spiritual—not social—process. He suggests that if we cultivate gratitude as a way of being, we may not change the world and its ills, but we can change our response to the world. If we fill our lives with moments of gratitude, we will indeed love the life we have.

978-1-57312-614-4 144 pages/pb **$15.00**

Choosing Gratitude 365 Days a Year
Your Daily Guide to Grateful Living

James A. Autry and Sally J. Pederson

Filled with quotes, poems, and the inspired voices of both Pederson and Autry, in a society consumed by fears of not having "enough"—money, possessions, security, and so on—this book suggests that if we cultivate gratitude as a way of being, we may not change the world and its ills, but we can change our response to the world.

978-1-57312-689-2 210 pages/pb **$18.00**

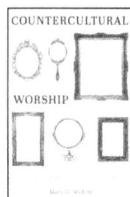

Countercultural Worship
A Plea to Evangelicals in a Secular Age

Mark G. McKim

Evangelical worship, McKim argues, has drifted far from both its biblical roots and historic origins, leaving evangelicals in danger of becoming mere chaplains to the wider culture, oblivious to the contradictions between what the secular culture says is real and important and what Scripture says is real and important.

978-1-57312-873-5 174 pages/pb **$19.00**

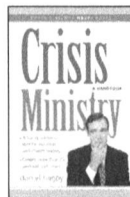

Crisis Ministry: A Handbook
Daniel G. Bagby

Covering more than 25 crisis pastoral care situations, this book provides a brief, practical guide for church leaders and other caregivers responding to stressful situations in the lives of parishioners. It tells how to resource caregiving professionals in the community who can help people in distress.

978-1-57312-370-9 154 pages/pb **$15.00**

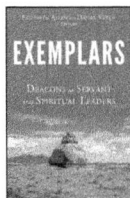

Exemplars
Deacons as Servant and Spiritual Leaders

Elizabeth Allen and Daniel Vestal, eds.

Who Do Deacons Need to Be? What Do Deacons Need to Know? What Do Deacons Need to Do? These three questions form the basis for *Exemplars: Deacons as Servant and Spiritual Leaders*. They are designed to encourage robust conversation within diaconates as well as between deacons, clergy, and other laity. 978-1-57312-876-6 128 pages/pb **$15.00**

The Exile and Beyond (All the Bible series)
Wayne Ballard

The Exile and Beyond brings to life the sacred literature of Israel and Judah that comprises the exilic and postexilic communities of faith. It covers Ezekiel, Isaiah, Haggai, Zechariah, Malachi, 1 & 2 Chronicles, Ezra, Nehemiah, Joel, Jonah, Song of Songs, Esther, and Daniel. 978-1-57312-759-2 196 pages/pb **$16.00**

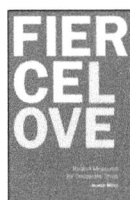

Fierce Love
Desperate Measures for Desperate Times

Jeanie Miley

Fierce Love is about learning to see yourself and know yourself as a conduit of love, operating from a full heart instead of trying to find someone to whom you can hook up your emotional hose and fill up your empty heart. 978-1-57312-810-0 276 pages/pb **$18.00**

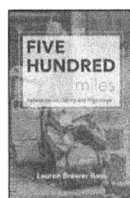

Five Hundred Miles
Reflections on Calling and Pilgrimage

Lauren Brewer Bass

Spain's Camino de Santiago, the Way of St. James, has been a cherished pilgrimage path for centuries, visited by countless people searching for healing, solace, purpose, and hope. These stories from her five-hundred-mile-walk is Lauren Brewer Bass's honest look at the often winding, always surprising journey of a calling. 978-1-57312-812-4 142 pages/pb **$16.00**

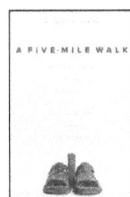

A Five-Mile Walk
Exploring Themes in the Experience of Christian Faith and Discipleship

Michael B. Brown

Sometimes the Christian journey is a stroll along quiet shores. Other times it is an uphill climb on narrow, snow-covered mountain paths. Usually, it is simply walking in the direction of wholeness, one step after another, sometimes even two steps forward and one step back.

978-1-57312-852-0 196 pages/pb **$18.00**

Glimpses from State Street

Wayne Ballard

As a collection of devotionals, *Glimpses from State Street* provides a wealth of insights and new ways to consider and develop our fellowship with Christ. It also serves as a window into the relationship between a small town pastor and a welcoming congregation.

978-1-57312-841-4 158 pages/pb **$15.00**

God's Servants, the Prophets

Bryan Bibb

God's Servants, the Prophets covers the Israelite and Judean prophetic literature from the preexilic period. It includes Amos, Hosea, Isaiah, Micah, Zephaniah, Nahum, Habakkuk, Jeremiah, and Obadiah.

978-1-57312-758-5 208 pages/pb **$16.00**

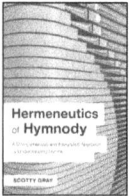

Hermeneutics of Hymnody
A Comprehensive and Integrated Approach to Understanding Hymns

Scotty Gray

Scotty Gray's *Hermeneutics of Hymnody* is a comprehensive and integrated approach to understanding hymns. It is unique in its holistic and interrelated exploration of seven of the broad facets of this most basic forms of Christian literature. A chapter is devoted to each and relates that facet to all of the others.

978-157312-767-7 432 pages/pb **$28.00**

Holy Hilarity
A Funny Study of Genesis

Mark Roncace

In this fun, meaningful, and practical study of Genesis, Mark Roncace brings readers fifty-three short chapters of wit and amusing observations about the biblical stories, followed by five thought-provoking questions for individual reflection or group discussion. Humorous, yet reverent, this refreshing approach to Bible study invites us, whatever our background, to wrestle with the issues in the text and discover the ways those issues intersect our own messy lives. It's seriously entertaining.

978-157312-892-6 230 pages/pb **$17.00**

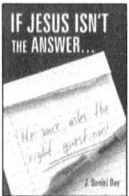

If Jesus Isn't the Answer . . . He Sure Asks the Right Questions!

J. Daniel Day

Taking eleven of Jesus' questions as its core, Day invites readers into their own conversation with Jesus. Equal parts testimony, theological instruction, pastoral counseling, and autobiography, the book is ultimately an invitation to honest Christian discipleship.

978-1-57312-797-4 148 pages/pb **$16.00**

Jonah (Annual Bible Study series)
Reluctant Prophet, Merciful God
Taylor Sandlin

The book of Jonah invites readers to ask important questions about who God is and who God calls us to be in response. Along with the prophet, we ask questions such as What kind of God is the God of Israel? and Who falls within the sphere of God's care? Most importantly, perhaps, we find ourselves asking How will I respond when I discover that God loves the people I love to hate? These sessions invite readers to wrestle with these questions and others like them as we discover God's mercy for both the worst of sinners and the most reluctant of prophets. *Teaching Guide 978-1-57312-910-7 164 pages/pb* **$14.00**

Study Guide 978-1-57312-911-4 96 pages/pb **$6.00**

Judaism
A Brief Guide to Faith and Practice
Sharon Pace

Sharon Pace's newest book is a sensitive and comprehensive introduction to Judaism. How does belief in the One God and a universal morality shape the way in which Jews see the world? How does one find meaning in life and the courage to endure suffering? How does one mark joy and forge community ties? *978-1-57312-644-1 144 pages/pb* **$16.00**

Live the Stories
50 Interactive Children's Sermons
Andrew Noe

Live the Stories provides church leaders a practical guide to teaching children during the worship service through play—and invites the rest of the congregation to join the fun. Noe's lessons allow children to play, laugh, and act out the stories of our faith and turn the sanctuary into a living testimony to what God has done in the past, is doing in the present, and will do in the future. As they learn the stories and grow, our children will develop in their faith. *978-1-57312-943-5 128 pages/pb* **$14.00**

Loyal Dissenters
Reading Scripture and Talking Freedom with 17th-century English Baptists
Lee Canipe

When Baptists in 17th-century England wanted to talk about freedom, they unfailingly began by reading the Bible—and what they found in Scripture inspired their compelling (and, ultimately, successful) arguments for religious liberty. In an age of widespread anxiety, suspicion, and hostility, these early Baptists refused to worship God in keeping with the king's command. *978-1-57312-872-8 178 pages/pb* **$19.00**

To order call **1-800-747-3016** or visit **www.helwys.com**

Meditations on Luke
Daily Devotions from the Gentile Physician
Chris Cadenhead

Readers searching for a fresh encounter with Scripture can delve into *Meditations on Luke*, a collection of daily devotions intended to guide the reader through the book of Luke, which gives us some of the most memorable stories in all of Scripture. The Scripture, response, and prayer will guide readers' own meditations as they listen and respond to God's voice, coming to us through Luke's Gospel. 978-1-57312-947-3 328 pages/pb **$22.00**

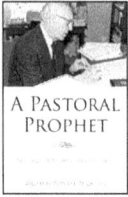

A Pastoral Prophet
Sermons and Prayers of Wayne E. Oates
William Powell Tuck, ed.

Read these sermons and prayers and look directly into the heart of Wayne Oates. He was a consummate counselor, theologian, and writer, but first of all he was a pastor. . . . He gave voice to our deepest hurts, then followed with words we long to hear: you are not alone.

—Kay Shurden
Associate Professor Emeritus, Clinical Education,
Mercer University School of Medicine, Macon, Georgia
978-157312-955-8 160 pages/pb **$18.00**

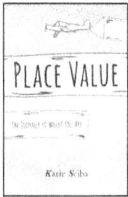

Place Value
The Journey to Where You Are
Katie Sciba

Does a place have value? Can a place change us? Is it possible for God to use the place you are in to form you? From Victoria, Texas to Indonesia, Belize, Australia, and beyond, Katie Sciba's wanderlust serves as a framework to understand your own places of deep emotion and how God may have been weaving redemption around you all along.
978-157312-829-2 138 pages/pb **$15.00**

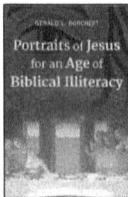

Portraits of Jesus
for an Age of Biblical Illiteracy
Gerald L. Borchert

Despite our era of communication and information overload, biblical illiteracy is widespread. In *Portraits of Jesus*, Gerald L. Borchert assists both ministers and laypeople with a return to what the New Testament writers say about this stunning Jesus who shocked the world and called a small company of believers into an electrifying transformation.
978-157312-940-4 212 pages/pb **$20.00**

Preaching that Connects
Charles B. Bugg and Alan Redditt

How does the minister stay focused on the holy when the daily demands of the church seem relentless? How do we come to a preaching event with a sense that God is working in us and through us? In *Preaching that Connects*, Charles Bugg and Alan Redditt explore the balancing act of a minister's authority as preacher, sharing what the congregation needs to hear, and the communal role as pastor, listening to God alongside congregants.   978-157312-887-2 128 pages/pb **$15.00**

Reading Isaiah
(Reading the Old Testament series)
A Literary and Theological Commentary
Hyun Chul Paul Kim

While closely exegeting key issues of each chapter, this commentary also explores interpretive relevance and significance between ancient texts and the modern world. Engaging with theological messages of the book of Isaiah as a unified whole, the commentary will both illuminate and inspire readers to wrestle with its theological implications for today's church and society.

978-1-57312-925-1 352 pages/pb **$33.00**

Reading Jeremiah
(Reading the Old Testament series)
A Literary and Theological Commentary
Corrine Carvalho

Reflecting the ways that communal tragedy permeates communal identity, the book of Jeremiah as literary text embodies the confusion, disorientation, and search for meaning that all such tragedy elicits. Just as the fall of Jerusalem fractured the Judean community and undercut every foundation on which it built its identity, so too the book itself (or more properly, the scroll) jumbles images, genres, and perspectives.   978-1-57312-924-4 186 pages/pb **$32.00**

Ruth & Esther (Smyth & Helwys Bible Commentary)
Kandy Queen-Sutherland

Ruth and Esther are the only two women for whom books of the Hebrew Bible are named. This distinction in itself sets the books apart from other biblical texts that bear male names, address the community through its male members, recall the workings of God and human history through a predominately male perspective, and look to the future through male heirs. These books are particularly stories of survival. The story of Ruth focuses on the survival of a family; Esther focuses on the survival of a people.   978-1-57312-891-9 544 pages/hc **$60.00**

To order call **1-800-747-3016** or visit **www.helwys.com**

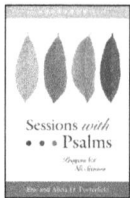

Sessions with Psalms (Sessions Bible Studies series)
Prayers for All Seasons
Eric and Alicia D. Porterfield

Useful to seminar leaders during preparation and group discussion, as well as in individual Bible study, *Sessions with Psalms* is a ten-session study designed to explore what it looks like for the words of the psalms to become the words of our prayers. Each session is followed by a thought-provoking page of questions. 978-1-57312-768-4 136 pages/pb **$14.00**

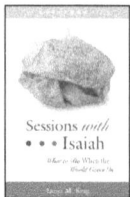

Sessions with Isaiah (Sessions Bible Studies series)
What to Do When the World Caves In
James M. King

The book of Isaiah begins in the years of national stress when, under various kings, Israel was surrounded by more powerful neighbors and foolishly sought foreign alliances rather than dependence on Yahweh. It continues with the natural result of that unfaithfulness: conquest by the great power in the region, Babylon, and the captivity of many of Israel's best and brightest in that foreign land. The book concludes anticipating their return to the land of promise and strong admonitions about the people's conduct—but we also hear God's reassuring messages of comfort and restoration, offered to all who repent.

978-1-57312-942-8 130 pages/pb **$14.00**

Stained-Glass Millennials
Rob Lee

We've heard the narrative that millennials are done with the institutional church; they've packed up and left. This book is an alternative to that story and chronicles the journey of millennials who are investing their lives in the institution because they believe in the church's resurrecting power. Through anecdotes and interviews, Rob Lee takes readers on a journey toward God's unfolding future for the church, a beloved institution in desperate need of change. 978-1-57312-926-8 156 pages/pb **$16.00**

Star Thrower
A Pastor's Handbook
William Powell Tuck

In *Star Thrower: A Pastor's Handbook*, William Powell Tuck draws on over fifty years of experience to share his perspective on being an effective pastor. He describes techniques for sermon preparation, pastoral care, and church administration, as well as for conducting Communion, funeral, wedding, and baptismal services. He also includes advice for working with laity and church staff, coping with church conflict, and nurturing one's own spiritual and family life. 978-1-57312-889-6 244 pages/pb **$15.00**

To order call **1-800-747-3016** or visit **www.helwys.com**

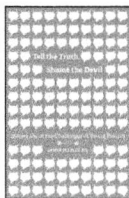

Tell the Truth, Shame the Devil
Stories about the Challenges of Young Pastors
James Elllis III, ed.

A pastor's life is uniquely difficult. *Tell the Truth, Shame the Devil*, then, is an attempt to expose some of the challenges that young clergy often face. While not exhaustive, this collection of essays is a superbly compelling and diverse introduction to how tough being a pastor under the age of thirty-five can be.   978-1-57312-839-1 198 pages/pb **$18.00**

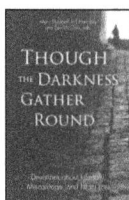

Though the Darkness Gather Round
Devotions about Infertility, Miscarriage, and Infant Loss
Mary Elizabeth Hill Hanchey and Erin McClain, eds.

Much courage is required to weather the long grief of infertility and the sudden grief of miscarriage and infant loss. This collection of devotions by men and women, ministers, chaplains, and lay leaders who can speak of such sorrow, is a much-needed resource and precious gift for families on this journey and the faith communities that walk beside them.

978-1-57312-811-7 180 pages/pb **$19.00**

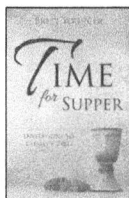

Time for Supper
Invitations to Christ's Table
Brett Younger

Some scholars suggest that every meal in literature is a communion scene. Could every meal in the Bible be a communion text? Could every passage be an invitation to God's grace? These meditations on the Lord's Supper help us listen to the myriad of ways God invites us to gratefully, reverently, and joyfully share the cup of Christ.   978-1-57312-720-2 246 pages/pb **$18.00**

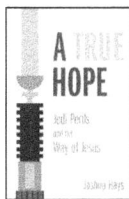

A True Hope
Jedi Perils and the Way of Jesus
Joshua Hays

Star Wars offers an accessible starting point for considering substantive issues of faith, philosophy, and ethics. In *A True Hope*, Joshua Hays explores some of these challenging ideas through the sayings of the Jedi Masters, examining the ways the worldview of the Jedi is at odds with that of the Bible.   978-1-57312-770-7 186 pages/pb **$18.00**

To order call **1-800-747-3016** or visit **www.helwys.com**

Clarence Jordan's

COTTON PATCH

Gospel

The
Complete
Collection

The Cotton Patch Gospel, by Koinonia Farm founder Clarence Jordan, recasts the stories of Jesus and the letters of the New Testament into the language and culture of the mid-twentieth-century South. Born out of the civil rights struggle, these now-classic translations of much of the New Testament bring the far-away places of Scripture closer to home: Gainesville, Selma, Birmingham, Atlanta, Washington D.C.

Hardback • 448 pages
Retail ~~50.00~~ • Your Price 25.00

Paperback • 448 pages
Retail ~~40.00~~ • Your Price 20.00

Clarence Jordan's
COTTON PATCH
Gospel
The
Complete Collection
INTRODUCTION BY JIMMY CARTER
Foreword by Will D. Campbell
Afterword by Tony Campolo

More than a translation, *The Cotton Patch Gospel* continues to make clear the startling relevance of Scripture for today. Now for the first time collected in a single, hardcover volume, this edition comes complete with a new Introduction by President Jimmy Carter, a Foreword by Will D. Campbell, and an Afterword by Tony Campolo. Smyth & Helwys Publishing is proud to help reintroduce these seminal works of Clarence Jordan to a new generation of believers, in an edition that can be passed down to generations still to come.

SMYTH&
HELWYS

To order call **1-800-747-3016**
or visit **www.helwys.com**

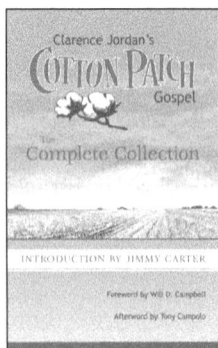

www.ingramcontent.com/pod-product-compliance
Lightning Source LLC
Chambersburg PA
CBHW052108090426
42741CB00009B/1730